CRAZY GOOD

A BOOK OF CHOICES

STEVE CHANDLER

MAURICE BASSETT

books for athletes of the mind

Crazy Good: A Book of CHOICES

Copyright © 2015 by Maurice Bassett

Maurice Bassett
P.O. Box 839
Anna Maria, FL 34216-0839

Contact the publisher:
MauriceBassett@gmail.com
www.MauriceBassett.com

Contact the author:
www.SteveChandler.com

Editing by Kathryn McCormick and Chris Nelson
Cover design by Carrie Brito

ISBN: 978-1-60025-034-7

Library of Congress Control Number: 2015914814

First Edition

To Kathy

Come do a little life with me . . .

~ Mo Pitney

The CHOICES

I shall be telling this with a sigh
Somewhere ages and ages hence:
Two roads diverged in a wood, and I—
I took the one less traveled by,
And that has made all the difference.

~ Robert Frost

Crazy good vs. Hard knock

Yes, to dance beneath the diamond sky
with one hand waving free,
silhouetted by the sea . . .

~ Bob Dylan
Mr. Tambourine Man

1

A flash goes up and down the spine

There is bad and there is good . . . And then there is crazy good.

Crazy good is something that goes so far beyond expectation that you've got goosebumps on your arms when you see it.

So imagine what it feels like to *live* it.

Most people (myself included, for most of my life) just ping-pong between bad and good. We are bad at something, and then we are good at something. And when we ping-pong over to good, it isn't even that good. We see it as fairly good, and most often it's just barely good enough.

But it never wakes the world up.

The world wakes up from something *so much better than it needs to be.* That's when the flash of astonishment goes up and down our spine.

I hesitate to give examples because you may not precisely agree with them. But you'll probably get the idea. (You can find your own versions of these once you get the idea.) These examples are my personal ones:

The Stones were good but the Beatles were crazy good. A

spring rain is good, but a thunderstorm is crazy good. *Ringling Brothers* was good, but *Cirque du Soleil* is crazy good.

Mobile telephones were good, but when Steve Jobs created the iPhone it was so much better than it had to be, so much cooler and more creative, that it was crazy good. Monet was good, but Van Gogh was crazy good. Elizabeth Bishop was good but Emily Dickinson was crazy good. Jack Nicholson's Joker was good, but Heath Ledger's was crazy . . . good. And so on.

Crazy good goes out beyond what anyone has anticipated. Like unexpected showers falling on a dried-out land. No one is really ready for the joy it brings.

2

The most interesting question ever

Now for the most interesting question ever. Here it is: Can your whole life become crazy good?

No matter who you are?

The answer I have found is almost too good to put into words.

Einstein said that the only question *he* really needed to know the answer to was: Is the universe friendly? He discovered (and his research had tremendous reach to it, no?) that it *was*. Others, too, have made the same discovery. When such an awakening came to G.K. Chesterton he described it as "absurd good news."

So how do we find that awakening ourselves? How do we get there?

I began my work as a coach by teaching people how to prevent going in the *opposite* direction of crazy good. I called it victim thinking. People who were able to identify and drop victim thinking made great gains in their lives.

But it wasn't until I was well into my fifties that I found out a person can do even better than that.

Certainly moving away from the victim mindset was

always reliably refreshing and energizing. But the real magic happened as I began to realize there was no upper limit to the life one could experience, or the creativity one could bring to this planet. And I mean anyone. As in everyone.

The path to that life, the crazy-good life, was a series of simple, clean and clear choices. They were choices that were hidden to most people, but once they were uncovered, anyone—you, even I—could easily make them.

3

It's a hard-knock life for me

For decades I thought I had experienced a hard-knock life. When I entered psychotherapy, I had it confirmed for me.

They gave me a soft bat to whack my parents with. Then they set out pillows for me to hit. One pillow was my mom and one was my dad.

It was kind of like a martial arts class. It cultivated my anger. Was that the objective? To make me more angry? To honor that feeling of anger?

I wasn't an orphan, exactly, like Annie, but I had two alcoholic parents. That's as many as you can have at any one time. Then, after I got married, my wife, the mother of my children, suffered from a severe mental disorder that institutionalized her and left me with full custody of four kids.

Not just kids, either. But wild and free little animals with rebellious spirits and bizarre forms of creativity that required some assistance from law enforcement for me to keep them whole. (Oh, I loved them. Almost too much. They taught me everything.)

I'm not finished here. With my victim story. I was an alcoholic myself! I forgot to tell you that. Victim of my parents' genes? Or maybe just a learned family tradition.

But fortunately I found recovery before any of the kids were born. I still go to Twelve-Step meetings with one of my children.

What am I leaving out? Oh yes, bankruptcy. That, too. Twenty-five years ago, but it still rings in my ears. Like tinnitus. Which I also have.

So, okay, that was my basis for thinking I was a victim. I nurtured and reinforced my victim mindset in adulthood. It was a hard-knock life, and I never learned to be happy.

Until I did.

And that's what led to my profession. Now I teach others, through coaching, how to drop the victim act and get on an evolutionary path. The journey of the human spirit. The road less travelled.

And one might ask, given my startling lack of success as a human being most of my life, why I am making a good living at this. I think it's because people realize that if I can do this, they certainly can. They easily can! So they hire me and I coach them. Our objective? A life that leaves the victim mindset behind, and then spirals up, flourishing, evolving, toward crazy good.

4

A lonely cell, my only hell

Part of my own path was to look back and see that everything I used to complain about in my past was actually there for my benefit. That rather than thinking I had a hard victim's life, I now realized that I had a fulfilling, encouraging adventure full of challenges—right out of the adventure comics and books I used to escape into so I wouldn't have to face life. I thought I was a victim of real life, so I escaped into fantasy life, reading about Superman and Robin Hood. If I had been one of those comic book characters they would have called me Victim Hood.

Most people, including those I coach, have painted a similar hard-knock life inside their own minds.

The song "It's the Hard-Knock Life" from the musical *Annie* refers to the tough situations and circumstances that the little orphans were up against. Later Jay-Z rapped out a hip-hop version of the same song in a more adult context. Featuring what *he* thought he was up against. ("Fleein' the murder scene, you know me well, from nightmares of a lonely cell, my only hell.")

Seeing life as full of hard knocks is the most common and widespread perception of life. I referred to it as "victim thinking" in an earlier book, and that whole book circled around just how automatic victim thinking had become for most people on this planet. (People believing they were lost and afraid in a world they never made.)

But because it's so conditioned, so pounded in, so deeply ingrained, it's hard to call it a conscious choice to think that way. It's more like a family tradition. A tradition of the human family. It's more like a hypnotized, knee-jerk response to everything. A *default setting* in the mind.

We are blind to it most of our lives, and then something beautiful happens and we can see. And once we see, we can't un-see. Which is cool, to put it mildly.

What do we see? What do we wake up to?

We wake up to the choices.

It's in these choices that we regain our power.

I may be stuck in victim thinking, temporarily, but if I step back and breathe I can see that I don't have to be. I don't have to believe the victim thoughts. I don't have to see my life through hard-knock glasses.

I can choose freedom, and if I choose freedom enough times, my life becomes better than good. It flies out there *beyond* good.

5

Believing her victim thoughts

I had this client once named Amanda.

(I call her "Amanda" to give her some privacy, even though she has told me I can share anything that might help. I'll just share a part of my time with her.)

I told Amanda that her troubles with money and men were a result of thoughts she was believing and certain choices she was not making.

"I get what you're saying intellectually," Amanda said. "But I don't really get it down here yet—on the cellular level—or in my heart."

Amanda pointed to her forehead when she said "intellectually" and then to her heart when she said "cellular level."

I said, "I might disagree with you. I think you *don't* get this intellectually. If you got it—really got it—intellectually, you'd have it. It would ring clear and true and you'd never lose it. So let's keep talking about it."

She couldn't see yet where she was automatically believing her negative victim thoughts without challenging them at all, without even holding them up to the light (like twenty-dollar bills) and looking to see if they were counterfeit.

Amanda thought people were unfair to her. They didn't listen to her. (My first psychotherapist would have started putting the pillows out and placing the soft bat in Amanda's hands right here.)

Other people disappointed her and let her down. Someone even "betrayed" her. She had missed a lot of opportunities in life. She didn't have a lot of the advantages other people had. She was certainly not treated well in her relationships with the pigs who called themselves men.

You can see that inside Amanda's mind this was a hard-knock life, filled with disappointment. She certainly felt like a victim, and given what she was believing, I couldn't blame her for feeling that way. We always feel what we think. No way out of that!

Amanda had never thought to challenge any of her negative thoughts. She believed that the test of whether a thought (no matter how frightening or negative) was true was *whether she herself was thinking that thought.* The ultimate test, right?

Once her thoughts were seen for what they were—just passing thoughts, like fleeting clouds—she opened her mind to a world of infinite possibilities. She was like a kid again.

6

Dying from alcohol and morphine

I sent Amanda a link to the Hank Williams, Jr. song, "Family Tradition." I invite you now to set this book down and go to YouTube and play that song and float around inside its message.

In Hank's song he asks himself why he is ruining his own life. He sings, "Hank, why do you drink? Why do you roll smoke?" and then he asks us to put ourselves in his "unique position. If I get stoned and sing all night, it's a family tradition."

Of course he's referring to his famous father, country legend Hank Williams, who died quite young of an overdose of alcohol and morphine. He was famous for "Your Cheating Heart," and his last single was prophetically called, "I'll Never Get Out of this World Alive."

Amanda said, "I don't see what this has to do with how I've been living. I'm not like a drunken fake cowboy who sings."

She was right about that. But addiction was addiction and Amanda was addicted to her victim stories and the morphine-like downer she experienced when she thought about her past life. However none of her thoughts and beliefs about money or men or life were original. She picked up most of the beliefs growing up in her family. None of her beliefs really had anything to do with the truth about life, and they were all dragging her down.

"I guess I need to replace my negative beliefs with more positive thoughts," she said. "Maybe we should start with money. I picked up a lot of frightening beliefs about money growing up in my family. In my house, whenever money was mentioned, fear filled the air. People would yell and scream. And *that* was a family tradition for sure."

I had asked Amanda in an earlier conversation who she thought had a crazy-good life in this world. She named a few people, and they all had big money in common. So I knew money meant a lot to her in both negative and positive ways.

But I had a question for her. Why did she want to create positive beliefs about money? What if she simply had no beliefs at all about money? What if she, unburdened by belief, could just let money flow in and out? Wouldn't that be pure freedom? Nothing to maintain. Nothing to feed and care for.

"Why is neutral better than positive?" she said.

"Because *your* positive has to be forced. And neutral can just be."

I asked if she was open to seeing money the same way she saw paint. It's just something that's often useful. But nothing you have to maintain a belief in one way or another. When you decide to paint the walls in your bedroom, you figure out how much paint you need and you go to the store and get the paint. Do you need positive beliefs about the paint? No, because paint is just paint. It's all right the way it is. It's perfect because it's neutral. It doesn't have to be given some hyped-up affirmative shock charge in your mind.

It would not be useful to try to force a positive belief in paint. To say an affirmation like, "Oh, paint! Divine paint.

Paint is the liquid manifestation of my expressive soul."

What if you got yourself to believe that, and then you spilled a bucket of paint? Instead of just getting a new bucket of paint, you'd have to deal with watching the liquid manifestation of your expressive soul running all over the floor! That would take a long time to process. You would definitely have feelings around that.

So, therefore, just realize that money is only money. It can be useful to you without all the moaning, noise, tears and dreams about it.

"But . . ." said Amanda. "It wouldn't do any harm to have a positive affirmation I say about money every day in order to create a new belief."

What Amanda wasn't seeing is that loading the mind up with beliefs, positive and negative alike, burden it and make life unnecessarily heavy and hard to walk through (much less dance with). It is the *clear* mind that enjoys a life that's out beyond good.

Amanda found, over time, that there were choices available to her that could free her from her serious life, full of heavy beliefs. Through these choices, she would become more light-hearted when she thought of things like money and men. And from that light-hearted state of mind, she would be able to enjoy life however it showed up.

Now we will look at the rest of the choices that Amanda (and I, and so many others) can discover and re-discover—and use.

SECOND CHOICE

Choosing vs. Trying to decide

Why in the world are we here?
Surely not to live in pain and fear.
Why on earth are you there,
when you're everywhere?

~ **John Lennon**
Instant Karma

1

How you can lose your marbles

I can spend forever trying to decide something.

The variables worth considering are infinite. I will never run out of variables to study. And so valuable time is lost. Not only that, but my mood declines the whole time I am trying to decide.

That's me in the corner. I sit on the floor, like a child with his spilled marbles, lost among the variables. Losing my spirit as the world passes me by. I would have been better off just *choosing something right off*, one of the options that felt right at the time, and going with it, to hell with the consequences.

Trying to figure out whether something is a "good decision" ahead of time can become an endless thought-maze to wander into. Besides, whether the decision is a "good one" is something I have a lot to say about *after* making the choice. If I choose to take a certain job, it's my work at that job that can turn it into a good decision. I can *make it into* a good decision by what I do and create after the choice.

Trying to have it all figured out *before* I choose keeps me dancing with fear. Like those quarterbacks who never know who to throw to, so their feet are dancing in place, faster and faster, until they are leveled by a 340-pound professional opponent. On the sidelines, lying on a stretcher, they tell the team neurologist that they were having a difficult time deciding who to throw to or whether to just throw it away.

"Trying to decide" is a popular way of losing the moment. A way that leads to always thinking about life instead of living life. For a life to become crazy good, it has to be *lived.*

On the other hand, there is an option. It's called choosing! Choosing has a great thrill in it. That's why your body tells you it's the better way to go.

Your life can be thrilling, or it can be endlessly debated in your mind.

And it's so fun when you find out that you can choose.

Recently I went to a very enjoyable concert in which I heard the rocking jazz band of Hugh Laurie, the star of the TV series *House*. Hugh Laurie is actually a British actor who plays blues piano and sings and chooses whatever career excites him at the moment. He just jumps right in, ready or not.

In an interview he said, "It's a terrible thing in life to wait until you're ready. I have this feeling now that actually no one is ever ready to do anything. There is almost no such thing as ready. There is only now."

2

You want it in the bag or with you?

Trying to decide things can take you right out of the flow of life. Whereas choosing moves things right along.

I am at the bookstore and I have just bought two books. There is a long line of people behind me and the counter lady is asking me whether I want my receipt with me or whether I want her to put it in the bag with the books.

"I don't know," I say, trying to decide which makes more sense.

She looks at me and raises her eyebrows.

I look back at her.

I say, "What do you suggest?"

"Sir, it's up to you."

"Well what is the downside of my just putting it in my pocket? Will someone be inspecting the bag?"

"No, sir," she says. "So I'll just give it to you, then." And she holds the receipt out for me to take.

"Wait a minute," I say, pulling my hand away. "I'm thinking the bag might be a better place for me to have it. Right? But really I'm not certain of that."

"Sir, please . . ."

"Do you mind if I call my wife? She knows about these kinds of things and it will just take a second."

"Would you please step out of line?"

"Yes, sure. But should I leave the receipt with you until I decide where I'm going to put it? Or should I hold it? What do you think, maybe give it to another customer to hold for us until I reach my wife? Her phone seems to be busy."

I get home later and notice that I can't find the receipt anywhere.

3

What should I commit myself to?

My friend Martha once watched a Steve Hardison video on the nature of commitment. She was moved and persuaded that his vision of commitment had irresistible power in it. But she had a vital question. She wanted to know, "How do I know what to commit to?"

So she asked Hardison.

His answer was simple. He said, "Choose."

4

How to get the goose
out of the bottle

I listen to Alan Watts audios all the time for entertainment and enlightenment. On one of them I remember that he tells a story about when he was once visited by a Chinese Zen master. Watts had his little daughter with him. The master decided to present them with a Zen koan, one of those unsolvable puzzles the masters liked to challenge their students with.

He said, "Once upon a time, there was a man who kept a very small goose in a bottle. And it began to grow larger and larger until he couldn't get it out of the bottle. Now, he didn't want to break the bottle, and he didn't want to hurt the goose, so what should he do? What would you do if you couldn't break the bottle, but you had to get the goose out of the bottle?"

Alan himself didn't have an answer to that, but his daughter did.

She said immediately, "Just break the bottle."

The Zen master turned to Watts and said, "You see, they always get it when they're under seven."

THIRD CHOICE

Verb vs. Noun

Dance me to your beauty
with a burning violin.
Dance me through the panic
till I'm gathered safely in.

~ **Leonard Cohen**
Dance Me to the End of Love

1

You must think you're something

So what are you choosing to *be* in life?

Are you being a verb or are you a noun?

Now if you don't remember your grammar (many of us don't want to remember our grammar) let me remind you that a noun is a person, a place, or a thing. It is something. It is an entity. It is a solid object that you can describe. Is that you?

Most people want to be that noun! They try to sell you on that concept, that they are a separate thing, apart from everything else. Flying solo. (Actually, sitting solo. Living solo.) But it's only a concept. It's only a belief. What's the reality?

Well, a more accurate understanding (a stronger choice) than the concept that you are a noun (or a thing) is that you are a verb! You are energy, action and movement. Verbs move. They dance, they sing, they embrace other people. They smile, they laugh, and they communicate. That's what verbs do.

Nouns are just there. Until you somehow motivate them, they just sit there.

Nouns have enablers that keep them in the noun state.

They are called adjectives—descriptors.

This is starting to sound a little like English class, but please stay with me, because many people, including myself, have had an AHA! in understanding the possibilities of a crazy-good life based on realizing that *in truth I am a verb.*

2

Am I that kind of person?

I received an email from Amanda that asked me whether I thought she was generous.

She was worried. Maybe she wasn't generous enough as a person to really utilize a service-based system I had taught her for acquiring clients.

"I just don't know that I'm a very generous person," she said, reflecting on the noun she thought she was. Was that noun generous?

I had been working with her for quite some time and that's why she felt I could pass judgment on this. Notice that she was testing an adjective (generous) to describe her noun (herself).

I was not willing to further the myth that she was a noun. I was not going to reinforce her perception of herself as being an entity, an identity, or a thing. I was going to help her get into *action*, if that was what she wanted to do. I was going to help her move from noun to verb because that's where all the fun is.

So my answer to her question was simply, "What act of generosity would you like to perform?"

"Oh," she said. And then she told me the action she was resisting taking. We saw a way to take it.

Why would I want to participate with her in labeling her and limiting her with the labels—you're generous, you're not generous, you're kind, you're not kind, you're courageous, you're cowardly, you're organized, you're disorganized. None of these things help anybody. None of them are even accurate for more than one or two seconds before everything changes. Life itself is nothing but changes. Change is another word for life.

Why not celebrate the great dance of interconnectivity?

Our breathing takes in oxygen from the plants. And that dance of breath makes us inseparable from the plants and the earth and all other things we are moving and dancing with whether we see it or not! Why do we try to freeze ourselves into feeling like static, disconnected objects?

What Amanda really is is a verb, and that's good. That's crazy good. That is Amanda at her best. And so by asking what act of generosity she would like to perform she could move out of her static, stuck position. No longer was she trying to figure out how to describe herself, trying to decide what she was really like.

Now anything was possible.

You will want to find the verb in you if you are going to live a wonderful life. Because the verb in you is who you really are. All the cells flowing and dancing through your system, all the atoms dancing inside of every molecule, all the molecules dancing in the cell—even *you* dancing as a great song comes to your ears and you feel you *just have to* get up and move—that's the real you.

3

Stupid was her favorite adjective

Amanda sometimes tried to convince me (and herself) that many of the things she did were stupid.

"I never should have taken that job. It was stupid."

Or: "I should have saved some of that money I made. Not doing that was really stupid."

And, "It was stupid of me to have hired that person without checking him out more thoroughly."

How easy to write these things off as stupid. How abrupt and dismissive. Just plain stupid. End of story. No more discussion.

Except for one tiny detail: Amanda was not stupid. Amanda was really smart.

So stupid didn't pass the test.

It was a cover story. It was too mindlessly easy.

And by being in the habit of labeling certain unwise actions and choices as "stupid," Amanda had no access to getting better and eliminating these mistakes.

Because how do you fix stupid? Make yourself smarter? What if you're already smart?

That looped-in stupid cul-de-sac was a convenient disposal in which Amanda could place every unwise choice. I wanted to help her see that she was not being truthful and that it was safe to come out of hiding on this matter.

"I never should have hired that man," she said. "It was stupid of me to think he would change. I thought at least he would stop drinking and gambling so much."

"Not stupid," I said. "Not stupid at all."

She was not agreeing with me. "It was *very* stupid," she insisted. "What else would you call it?"

"Unwise and undisciplined," I said.

For years I had a quote up on my office wall that said, "Only the disciplined are free." It was there to remind me. My old way of thinking was that "only the disciplined are neo-Nazi boring."

I wanted Amanda to see that wisdom and discipline are partners. They go together. And every "stupid" mistake she regretted was something that a little more wisdom and a lot more discipline would have avoided.

I asked her about the hiring mistake she made. How much research had she done into the person's background. More important, how many hours had she spent interviewing him? (To research and to interview are verbs.)

"Very little," said Amanda. "Not much. We were in a bind. I hoped I'd get lucky. I didn't have time to do a long interview. Or so I thought. Really stupid."

Not stupid. Undisciplined and unwise.

"What does it matter what negative label I give it?" she said. "Who cares if it's stupid or undisciplined?"

I cared because I was committed to helping her get a better life—and only because that was what *she* was committed to. I wanted her to see that there were always things she could do, actions she could take. She didn't have to stay a noun and paste "stupid" stickers all over that noun.

"Stupid you can't fix," I said. "Stupid is just stupid. There's nowhere you can go from there."

She finally nodded. She got out her notebook. Always a good sign.

She said, "Whereas undisciplined is something I can adjust."

Yes. Exactly.

She could put in a discipline, a gentle routine. (Many people shy away from the thought of discipline because they think it's too harsh—but it can be gentle and relaxed.) Her new discipline would require a good background check and at least two very long interviews before hiring anyone.

Amanda began to phase out stupid in her life. She saw that stupid is something that describes a paralyzed noun. She stopped labeling things that way. If she thought it was stupid for her to lose her car keys and not have a backup set (which actually happened) she resisted calling it stupid. She just put in a new discipline moving forward. A discipline is something a verb can act on.

FOURTH CHOICE

Creating vs. Reacting

Love and gravity are why we fall,
and life's deepest meaning is:
it's short. That's all.

~ Fred Knipe
Love and Gravity

1

This guy needs to be taught a lesson

I receive a negative, nasty email.

Someone hates me. That's my first thought.

So then I think revenge. How could I be hated? How can that be? My ego has to be protected from that, even though I know, deep down, that my ego is, as Ken Wilber says, *kept in existence* by a collection of emotional insults. Still. What would be a clever put-down? How can I humiliate this idiot and show him he should not be messing with me at this level, words against words?

This guy said he'd purchased one of my very first audio programs and it was awful. It was worse than awful. My voice was so slow and monotonous he couldn't stand it.

"It made me want to kill myself," he said.

Wow. That's a heavy criticism.

So . . . How should I defend myself?

I start to compose a reply. I'll tell him that only idiots want what he wants—some ranting and raving motivational type guy who spits spittle from a red face hyped with passion popping out of it. Some raving secular evangelist selling a speed-rap of monetized passion.

I'll say my audio is for thoughtful people, so I speak slowly. I'll tell him I put a lot of time into my words. I don't want to insult the listener by sounding like I'm in a shouting contest. I'll say if you need to be motivated by the tone of someone's voice, by the urgency in their screeching throat, then you are in a self-induced coma. You are not an awakened human being. Stay away from me or I'll have you locked up.

I back away from the keyboard before I send all that.

I see that I'm *reacting*.

I start to worry about how upset I've made myself and how it will impact the work I have to do. I am now considering cancelling some of my work today. Then my anger turns from hot to cold. I've worn myself out, mentally. I've descended from wired-up to just mildly unraveled. I am slumping in my chair. I re-read his words.

Then I realize I have a choice. I don't have to *react* to this guy. I can do the opposite.

If only I can remember the opposite.

What is the opposite of reacting? Oh, right! Creating! I can create. Reacting and creating have the exact same letters in them. That helps me remember.

Deep breath. Okay. What do I want to create?

How about I create a relationship? Why not shoot for that? I could create a bond with him, maybe, based on my desire to serve people. Am I shooting for the moon with that? So what? President Kennedy got a lot of mileage out of shooting for the moon.

But we're not off to a good start, this guy and me, I have to acknowledge that. Am I even sure he's still alive? He said he felt like killing himself after listening to me.

I'm sure that was just an expression. Okay. I will see what

I can create.

So I write back. I decide to be completely honest.

I say, "Dear Harmon," (because his name is Harmon) "I hear you. In fact, I agree with you. My early recordings are just flat out bad. I think the current ones are getting better, but I could be fooling myself. I have to say I appreciate people like you who have the courage to reach out and tell me the truth. You are helping me get better. I am sorry for your negative experience and I want to make it up to you. If you send me your mailing address, I'll send my two latest books to you. You can read those to yourself at your own chosen speed. Thanks for taking the time to communicate with me."

This is my response to Harmon. A few days go by and I get an email from him: "Well, that was unexpected. I must say you take criticism pretty well. Was I too negative? I do like your books. Did I tell you that? I enjoy reading them."

I send two books out to him. A relationship is being created. Created! In the old days I would have just gone with my first reaction.

2

Coloring the world with my mood

Moods are like blobs of paint on a palette.

Once I react to something, I drop down into a bad mood. Then I try to describe what's going on. But the only paints I have to paint the picture with are the gloomy paints of a low mood. So innocent situations look like unbelievable challenges when I put them up there on the canvas. Ordinary, everyday events get painted as catastrophes. In that low mood "life sucks," as our celebrities and children say.

But what if I stop reacting and start creating? What if I just start noticing when I am reacting? What if I then back away and breathe? "Given this situation, what can I create?" What if I just start doing that as a practice? Almost like a hobby that I get more and more into?

Would there be any problems left?

3

How could a problem be good?

Peter Diamandis says, "I think of problems as gold mines."

He is the successful founder of more than fifteen high-tech companies.

Just that thought gets my own creativity going. How could this problem be a gold mine?

My coach Steve Hardison trained me in this always-available choice between creating and reacting. He is like Diamandis! I realize now that Steve, too, sees problems as gold mines.

I sit down with him for a coaching session and tell him my latest problem. He listens carefully and compassionately and I see his eyes start to sparkle. I can start to feel his impatience with me as I keep trying to finish my story about my problem. He is about to come out of his chair and embrace me with creative joy. I see once again that problems excite him.

After I finish talking he asks me a simple question, "Given what is happening, what would you like to create?"

But when I'm in a low mood, I don't always immediately warm up to that line of questioning. What is this, art class? Am I back in kindergarten with finger-paints? Should we get out the Legos?

Yes, Yes and Yes.

4

Now live your life as a poet

The poet Pablo Neruda used to write his poems in green ink!

He said the green ink was his own playful symbol for desire and hope. Which I thought was charmingly childlike for a writer of his stature and fame. He said, "A child who does not play is not a child, but the man who doesn't play has lost forever the child who lived in him and who he will miss terribly."

I would have missed my own child terribly if I'd never been re-introduced to *creating* (an activity that comes so naturally to the child). But now I know the option for creating is always there. It exists inside every moment, every problem. Every time I catch myself reacting.

5

How can being in love be easy?

Many years ago I was experiencing a problem in my relationship with Kathy. As much as I loved her and enjoyed her company, we were having difficulties harmonizing and combining our lives. We lived miles apart. We had different jobs. Were we starting to drift apart, given the logistical challenges?

If so, it was a problem.

I took the problem into a session with my coach, Steve Hardison. He listened, and then he said, "What would you like to create?"

And I had a hard time answering. I finally said, "I don't know. A closer relationship? Some kind of system for more time together? Something like that?"

He was silent for awhile. Unusual for him. I waited. I began to think that maybe this "What would you like to create?" thing might not always apply. It might have hidden limitations. Maybe some things, like relationships, are too complex for such a simple choice. There are nuances in a relationship! No one can deny that. Subtleties, too! My mind was fading out.

Then he said, "What do you want?"

I thought I'd answered that question. A new system? I was confused.

He said, "In the long run, what do you want from her? Do you want to get married?"

I thought yes, so I said, "Oh yes, absolutely. Someday."

"Someday?" he said. "What someday? Which one?"

"Excuse me?"

"What day? When?"

"I don't know, how would I know?"

"Who else would know? Who else knows what you want?"

"Okay I see that . . . right."

He said nothing.

Then he said, "Do you want to do some creating right now?"

"Yes."

Then he reached into a drawer behind him and pulled out a very large calendar and spread it out in front of us.

He said, "Let's create, okay? Let's choose a month. Are you game? Just for the fun of it."

"Sure."

And after looking for a minute I chose November of the following year. That would be a great time to get married to Kathy. He lit up.

"Perfect!" he said. "I can't wait to be there! Are you ready to ask her, to talk to her, to tell her?"

I hesitated, but not for very long. Now I was excited, too. Can you do this? Can you just create a life like this? I was thinking of how much I loved Kathy and how right this all felt.

Hardison smiled and said, "We have a few minutes left. What else do you want to work on today?"

"You're kidding, right?"

Kathy and I were married that next November—the same November I pointed to on Hardison's calendar. (It turned out that Kathy, too, had also secretly preferred that very month.) Hardison was my best man at the wedding. It was a huge and beautiful wedding, thanks to Kathy, who created all the details. I love this memory. So:

Here's to Kathy:

I leave this note by your pillow. I set it down without a sound.
The note has just two words. The words are: paradise found.

FIFTH CHOICE

Something vs. Nothing

You know who I am,
you've stared at the sun.
Well, I am the one who loves changing
from nothing to one.

~ Leonard Cohen
You Know Who I Am

1

I remember the time I just fell apart

I used to be nothing.

In my own mind.

I was nothing in certain important categories. Like courage, productivity, responsibility. Things like that.

I would set out to change. From nothing to something. But it never worked. It was during the time when I had a family, and I was learning to live sober and . . .

. . . then I just fell apart, psychologically, while trying to run a business I owned. I was raising four children on my own and trying to understand why their mother had been institutionalized in a maximum-security-suicide-watch wing of a mental hospital in Tucson.

"She has severe dissociative disorder," her doctor told me. "The disorder is what you would know, from the movies, as multiple personality."

From the *movies*? Her doctors are referring me to the movies? For stability and reassurance? Like *Sybil*? Like *Three Faces of Eve*?

Fun.

Not really. Especially for her. She lived, at that time, in a state of wild panic and confusion. My state was not as terrifying as hers, but I still needed help.

I asked the doctor where her disorder came from. I told him I had not seen any sign of it for our first six years together.

"She was abused, quite severely, as a child, by a satanic cult," he said. "Her memories of it had been successfully repressed until recently, but somebody contacted her, and something happened, we don't know, but the repression didn't hold. In effect, she came undone."

I felt for her. She was such a wonderful person. I felt for the children. But I wanted to not come undone myself so I looked for help.

2

My wild attempts at change

Please help me with this!

That's what I said to Dr. Nathaniel Branden as I told him about my wife's condition and my attempts to raise children on my own.

I had always loved Dr. Branden's books on psychology and self-esteem, so I'd called his office and made some phone appointments with him. After a very successful and encouraging series of phone psychotherapy sessions, I flew to L.A. and had sessions with him in person.

We talked about the foolishness of trying to change immediately and radically from nothing to something. From scared to confident. Instead, he taught me his 5% solution.

Dr. Branden had me give six rapid answers to the sentence stem, "If I were 5% more responsible for my life today . . ."

My answers, off the top of my head, were like these:

. . . then I would get more sleep.

. . . I would delegate more of my office work to my team.

. . . I'd read spiritual literature every morning.

. . . I'd meet with my children's teachers.

. . . I'd plan my day and week more thoughtfully.

. . . I'd ask for help more often.

He applied the same process to being 5% more peaceful inside, to being a 5% better parent, a 5% better husband, better provider, and on and on. It amazed me that the answers were always inside me, ready to pour out. They just needed some prompting and a kind of game to get it going.

By thinking in terms of a 5% improvement, my mind opened up easily. I saw all kinds of little things I could be doing immediately. I saw I could do anything 5% better, but to change something *completely* was frighteningly hard to think about.

I never appreciated the full genius in that until years later, when I began using the 5% question with my own clients.

3

No more false magic

The client I call Bradley was down on himself for having spent the past year in a "totally unproductive" way. He had a small business and he wasn't growing it as fast as he wanted to.

"I've been completely unproductive," he told me. He said he wanted me to help him change. He wanted this next year to be productive. He wanted to go from unproductive to productive. (From nothing to something! The doomed polarity!)

It wasn't going to work for him. Not that approach. Because having personal productivity appear out of nothing is false magic. It is not how real-world success works. Thanks to Dr. Branden, and my own experience, I now knew that.

I told Bradley we would only make progress if he was willing to see that he was already somewhat productive. Then we could go from productive to more productive. That's where the action would be. That's where all success lies— going from good to better and better, *not* trying to go from bad to good. Movement is always on a continuum. It's a learning curve, not a leap of faith.

"But I *am* unproductive!" Bradley said. "I don't want to

sugarcoat it!"

Compared to whom? I asked him to walk through the city's downtown park one day as part of our coaching session. I would point to a homeless person sitting on a piece of cardboard and I'd ask if he were more productive than that man.

"Of course," said Bradley, not getting it yet.

Then we walked past a t-shirt store that was boarded up and out of business. Bradley said he used to love that store.

"Were you more productive than they were last year?" I asked. He said yes, obviously. We walked on, and as I pointed out more examples he began to see. It was all relative. Thinking in dramatic polarities was not serving him. Maybe it was time to STOP THE DRAMA.

In our next session I asked him to list for me ten ways he *was* productive in the past year. He started slowly, but then had no trouble doing this. Then I asked him to list five people he knew personally who were *less* productive than he was in the past year. In his mind and memory he found those people quickly.

"Okay, okay," he said. "So I see what you're doing. I can't really truthfully say I am not productive."

I agreed. (Later I gave him a series of Byron Katie books to really learn the liberating power of self-inquiry.)

He said, "I'm just not nearly as productive as I want to be."

"Yes. Right. Good! Now we can work," I said. "Because now we can go from productive to more productive. That's your path."

It didn't take long for Bradley to find many ways he could be 5% more productive each day. And if you do the math, that adds up fast. He was doing the doable. He was not trying to conjure up a magical leap from nothing. Leaping from nowhere to leap from. That approach would leave him with no foundation, and without a leg to stand on.

4

He was pumping from a dry well

It used to be when people lived on farms water had to be pumped from the ground. By hand. If you were from the city and no one told you how it was done you might pump until you were red-faced and sweating.

And produce nothing but air!

Have you ever had that feeling? That nothing in your life was really working? That you were pumping air? I'll tell you truly: I have had that feeling.

This is what Bradley was doing. Pumping his psyche wearily. Producing emptiness and shame! Feeling shame at his inadequacy and then acting bewildered at the lack of results. Every stroke—every old disappointment—was adding more frustration.

I know that we all do this. (Until we don't.) We criticize ourselves. We think we're failures. We think that critical self-talk might shame us into *doing something*. But it doesn't. It just returns us to our emptiness.

Until we finally see how ineffective it is to even try that route.

The dry pump on the farm needs to be *primed*. With water. You need water to get water! Add a little water to the dry seals and pipes and the well water will begin to flow. Cool, sweet, deep well water. (Life itself.)

Brad needed to use some existing results to realize he could get future results, an apparent paradox. But it's not paradoxical. By adding past successes to our thinking, we began to get some water. No matter how small those achievements have been, they are enough to get a good life flowing.

5

I needed to make a big, magical leap

I used to think I had to do that magical leap myself.

If I was cowardly, I had to change completely into super courageous. If I was weak, I had to become amazingly strong. If I was overweight I had to become rail thin.

It never worked because it was a dysfunctional approach. It was a dream that divorced me from reality. I had no idea back then that reality was kind, and that reality was on my side, ready to work with me, ready to support me in everything.

Before Dr. Branden, I had always been stuck inside the innocent malfunction of using self-criticism as a motivator. But the problem with that is that after you condemn yourself as being wrong or bad you immediately disconnect yourself from reality.

Self-criticism is like pulling a lamp's plug out of the wall because it isn't giving the room enough light. But now the room goes completely dark.

Oops.

6

Just whose side are you on?

To produce something you have to start with something.

You have to see the good in who you already are.

You have to acknowledge that you've done the best you could so far, given what you've been believing and how you have seen your life.

You have to take that walk over to *your* side of the courtroom. So that you are no longer the prosecutor in your life. Now you're on *your* side. You are your own attorney. *You represent yourself from now on.*

Systems vs. Dreams

How beautiful to know
we create our own tragedies.

~ Nick Cave

1

If you can dream it you can do it

I don't want to say that dreams are a useless thing, because they are not. They are beautiful. They can be a guiding inspiration.

In fact I have encouraged a lot of people to dream. When they're feeling blue. I helped create a video for young people called *Do the Dream*, based on Walt Disney's famous philosophy, "If you can dream it, you can do it."

So dreams are good, right? A dream is a wish your heart makes. "Dream big!" many good people say.

But then what?

Okay, I'm dreaming big. I even have pictures all over my wall of what my dream is.

But one day I wake up in a low mood. I see the pictures and I want to tear them down. It all seems so far away. In fact my dream feels like it's mocking me. It's now seen in my mind as *that goal I haven't reached.*

When a dream becomes the goal I haven't reached, the journey I have not made, then it ceases to have a good effect on me. Quite the opposite. When I share that dream with other people they may even point out that it's a nice thought but I haven't been able to make my credit card payments this month and I'm slipping deeper into debt and failure.

And yet there's the dream on the wall. Reminding me of the not-accomplished. Making me feel worse. I'd be in a better, more productive mood if there was no dream at all up there. At least that's how I feel today. Bummer.

Fortunately I found an answer to all of this.

It happened six or seven years ago when I was asked to do some coaching and training for Microchip Technology. I learned their culture's operating principles by reading *Aggregate Systems*, the book by Steve Sanghi, their CEO. I had one of those moments. Aha. Bingo. Enlightenment.

"Every system is perfect," said Sanghi.

Okay? And?

"Every system is perfect for the result it gets. If you want a different result, put in a different system."

Oh, wow. That was a moment.

My system of not earning enough to pay my bills—*or*, of earning enough but spending it on other things—was perfect. It was perfect! (For the result it was getting. And that result was debt and worry and fear.)

Did I want a different result? Yes! Would it work to dream bigger? To put pictures of a castle in Spain on the wall? A castle where I would live in abundance? No. In fact, that castle would have ridiculed me and caused me to avert my eyes from it.

I simply needed a new system. A system that would be perfect for producing the result I wanted. A system I could jump into and benefit from every day because it was not *out there*, stranded in my future.

2

The dream that led to dysfunction

My friend Horst was a website consultant who wanted my help.

When he called me he began by saying that he had a real problem and didn't know how to solve it. I asked him what his problem was.

"I'm not a detail person," he said.

I asked him to explain.

"Well, I'm behind on my invoices. Someone will have a consultation with me, and I just don't invoice them and after a while it gets lost in the shuffle and I forget who owes me money."

I asked Horst what he thought the cause of his problem was.

"I told you," he said. "I'm not a detail person. I never have been."

"I don't think it's that," I said. "Because I don't like to recognize or acknowledge permanent personality traits that *cause* things to happen."

"Okay but this feels real, this detail thing. What *do* you recognize?"

"Systems," I said. "It's all about systems. Every system is perfect for the result it is getting. If you want a different result, put in a different system."

"But I don't have a system."

"Oh yes you do. Your system is to let the invoices fade into oblivion, hoping someday your personality will change. That system is getting you the result of disorder and chaos. It's perfect. It's a perfect system for the result."

"I've been hoping I'd change," said Horst. "You know I've been in therapy."

"Which is great. But—"

"My hope was I'd get to the bottom of my problem."

"A worthy dream," I said, "to find the bottom. And I have nothing against dreams, but meanwhile your clients aren't being invoiced and you aren't getting paid."

"Right. So what do you suggest?"

"A different system. One that works."

"Do you have one in mind?"

I really didn't, so I made one up on the spot.

My system was simple. The moment—the very moment— Horst finished a consultation, he was to create and send an invoice. He was not allowed to *do anything else* between the billable consult and the invoice, not even go to the bathroom. And this practice would have no exception to it, and could not be re-considered or second-guessed.

I said, "Use a catheter if you have to."

"Just so long as I do it every time," he said, lighting up.

"Yes, and notice that it won't matter whether you are a detail person or not. The system ignores all that."

Fortunately for Horst his system has held up, way beyond

the thirty days he agreed to track it for me.

Horst also learned the larger lesson: you can have an unfulfilled dream or you can have a system. Your choice.

His dream of some day becoming a "detail person"—whatever that is—was a fantasy that only served to deepen his overall sense of inadequacy.

His system, on the other hand, put him in touch with the infinite problem-solving power of the human spirit.

Serving vs. Pleasing

Honesty
is hardly ever heard,
and mostly what I need from you.

~ Billy Joel
Honesty

1

What pleases is not always what serves

When I was a desperate, suicidal alcoholic and I came to your home and you made me a strong drink, you were pleasing me.

If, instead, you took me to a Twelve-Step meeting you were serving me.

There is a big difference between pleasing and serving.

Once I was shopping for cars, and I'd visited a Ford dealership and a Chevy dealership. The Ford salesman was dedicated to serving. When he called me after my visit he reported that he had done extensive research on questions I'd asked about the car I was looking at. He'd put in some time, done some homework, and was calling to tell me what he found. The features he could add. That call was pure service.

The Chevy salesperson called, too, but there was no service. He was just "checking in" with friendly cheerful language, "touching base" with me and sounding very happy in an artificial way. Still looking for his sales commission.

I said, "So, why are you checking in?"

"Well, um, just to see if you got the tickets to the Ice

Capades I sent you."

"Yes. Thank you."

"Oh, de nada, sir, no worries! I wanted to check in and see. You're one of my favorite customers ever, so . . . be cool Mr. C!"

I said goodbye.

There is no substitute for true service. If I ask myself, "What would serve this person right now?" I always create a better communication than I would by simply trying to please.

Most people who sell for a living have a difficult time distinguishing between pleasing and serving. Their default setting is to try to be pleasing. So they flatter their customer, take them to lunch, buy little gifts, and put up a very phony show of happy friendship. Whereas the salesperson who tells the truth, does his homework and research and sincerely asks, "What would genuinely serve this person?" succeeds much faster.

We are taught from the age of two or three to be *pleasing*. We get praise for "being good" and not embarrassing our parents. We become skilled at it. When we grow older we learn to please the people in our peer group. So the practice continues. It never stops.

But as we enter the adventure of adulthood the automatic attempt to please people starts to work against us. We don't notice the gag reflex kicking in with the people we flatter. We soon begin to have a hard time telling people the truth. Our relationships suffer. Professionally, we start to have a hard time connecting.

So we buy Ice Capades tickets? We buy them bear claws?

We don't see it. These people haven't been served. Look at how they tend to drift away.

2

Pleasing was diluting my energy

"Hey, my friend, I'm passing through town and would like to take you to lunch!" said a person I barely know. "I know you're busy, but you have to eat, right? I'd love to pick your brain!"

Because back then I had no real clarity about the choice between pleasing and serving, I heard myself automatically saying yes. After all, I didn't want to be unpleasant!

But then I began resenting that "friend" all the days that led up to our lunch. I was behind in my work and now I'd be getting in my car and losing two hours out of my life I could never get back, all because I'd been automatically pleasing. I felt like a jerk. Just automatically saying yes all the time. I was a knee-jerk jerk.

What would have *served* my friend and me would have been honesty. I could have said, "No, I'm sorry, having lunch won't work. But it is good to hear from you and I really appreciate your asking me to lunch. That was thoughtful and kind of you. Did you say you had a question? Let's answer it now."

Most of my time-management problems have come from saying yes to too many people. My feeling "swamped" never came from my having a poor time-management program. It always came from too much pleasing.

3

Now the door is open to hell

I once worked for a media company in Tucson. The president never got his important leadership challenges solved. He was unable to steer his company out of increasing debt and despair.

Why? Pleasing.

His life was about pleasing people rather than serving them.

His door was always open! All day. You or anyone else could walk in with the smallest of problems or issues—or even just a restless urge to "chat." And he would come bounding out from behind his desk beaming with a huge smile and a welcoming handshake, gesturing toward a chair for you to sit in.

He would smile and chuckle all day as his company ran deeper into debt. Because he just could not say no. He could not stop himself from pleasing people all day long.

But his people were not being served. Service would have been strong leadership. Service would have had his door closed up tight as he solved the problems of the company. He would not need to be unkind or unfriendly. He would only have had to ask himself each day, "What would *serve* my people?" versus always *automatically* doing what would please them. He just couldn't help himself.

4

How dare she keep calling me all day?

When Amanda was trying to run a small company she owned and first wanted my help, it was because she was "in crisis," as she put it. She said she was completely disorganized, running around putting out fires all day. Fires, we would later find out, of her own making.

I asked her what got in the way of her having a relaxed, focused day. She told me it was interruption. She couldn't focus for even one minute without someone calling her. When I asked her to tell me who calls, she said, "Oh, everyone. Especially my mother."

"Your mother?"

"She calls me, and I'm not exaggerating, five or six times a day."

"Are those emergency calls?" I said. "Is she having health problems?"

"Well, no. Sometimes, but no, usually not."

"And your mother knows you are working during the day, running your business?"

"Yes!"

"Then why do you take her calls?"

"What do you mean?"

"Why do you interrupt your day to take her calls?"

"She's my mother!"

I said nothing.

She said, "I don't want to upset her. I guess I'm thinking if she's my mother I want to be there for her."

"But now you resent her."

"Yes. A lot."

"When you talk about her you're angry at how often she disturbs your day. You are not being honest with her."

"She wouldn't like that."

Amanda was pleasing her mother. No one was really being served. Her mother was not being told the truth, that her daughter had *work* to do. Amanda was allowing her days to slip into chaos because she thought her only choice, ever, was to please her mother. (And that was also true for all the other family members whose calls she took automatically.)

When she fully understood the option of *serving*, she created an agreement with her mother to talk briefly each day, but only after all her work was finished. At first her mother complained. She said she was feeling abandoned. She couldn't see that it was a service to her (and her daughter) to break this inappropriate, codependent bond during the day. But it eventually returned them both to the real world of honesty and compassion. It removed them both from the nightmarish cycle of pleasing and inevitable resentment.

When I say "yes" to everyone and everything I have a hard time keeping all those promises. Soon my life becomes a series of apologies, and then resentments. Yes, I even start blaming *them*. "How dare she call me all day when she knows full well I have a business to run!"

Saying "no" to people serves them. And me. It takes a lot of practice, but it gets easier and more enjoyable as I do more of it. It's the Michelangelo principle at work. Michelangelo would obtain a huge slab of marble and start chipping away. He would remove chunks of stone. And by taking things *away* what finally appeared was a beautiful statue.

5

Remember we used to get in trouble?

When we were young, we got in trouble for saying no. Sometimes when a parent or guardian told us to do something and we said, "No!" we would suffer grave consequences. Sometimes physical punishment.

"You don't say NO to *me*, young man!" and then WHACK!

It's hard to enjoy doing something that you used to get beaten for.

It requires a complete turnaround in mindset.

But if you do turn your mind around, you are happier. What gets freed up for you is beyond good. A life of creative, profound service. A life in which you, yourself, are being served, too. By having free time and space to breathe in.

6

If I only had a brain

We are programmed to please.

That's how we survive when we are little. That's how we created our personalities. The biological computer (the brain) gets programmed to please people. When we get out into adult life and we're now seeking to make a success of ourselves and have a good career, all that programming is *still there*.

And that's a problem.

Because then we go out into the world and all we know to do is to please people. But this time it doesn't work so well, because when adults try to please other adults, it's not so welcome. So it doesn't create true relationships or move your career along. It's usually looked at as apple-polishing, or bootlicking (or worse), and it confuses people. And yet the programming is *still in there*, running the brain, trying to please.

In order to spiral up toward crazy good we have to re-program.

7

The deathbed question

I like people to imagine their upcoming deathbed experience.

What will happen when you are on your deathbed looking back on your life? Will you ask yourself, "How many people have I pleased? Did I really please people? Did I win enough of them over?"

Probably not. Those won't be the questions you'll ask yourself on that deathbed. Really what is asked on the deathbed is this: "Who have I served? What difference have I made? What difference has my life made? Is life different because I was here on earth?"

That's what people truly wonder. They don't wonder how many people they pleased. How many people they maneuvered into liking them. What they think of is this: Who did I serve? Did I spend my days serving? Yes or No. And if the answer's yes, what a beautiful feeling.

EIGHTH CHOICE

Game vs. Shame

You know drinking alone's a shame.
It's a shame, it's a crying shame.
Look at those jokers glued to that
damn hockey game.

~ Joni Mitchell
Raised on Robbery

1

Maybe I can shame myself into it

I am starting to get down on myself again. That's never a good thing. When I get down on myself like this I really feel like doing nothing. Maybe turning on ESPN to see if some sports team is doing something interesting. Anything to distract me from the shame.

Then I remember.

There is always another way I can motivate myself. I don't have to stay in this one way, this shame-based way.

ESPN reminds me: I could start a game.

Why is that so hard to remember? Maybe it's because shame seems to be *everyone's* motivation of choice. I'll shame myself into doing this thing. By talking to myself this way: "Stop fooling around. You know what successful people do? They get down to work. They grow up."

And to get this system going faster, I'll dust off the old reliable word SHOULD.

Shame says I *should have*. Shame says, "I should have an organized desk, I should be more like that person," and the shame-based SHOULDS keep piling up.

Why doesn't this approach work? (If it worked we'd all be

very active and fulfilled throughout the day.)

But how *could* it work? When you consider how it makes us feel? This vague sense of being ashamed of ourselves. And soon a new low: complete discouragement.

Discouragement! Oh now I'm really low. And it's such an interesting word when you look at it. I am **dis**sing the courage in me. Discouragement is a sad place to be. Hard to generate any energy from that place.

My observation is that about 80% of us use this shaming system. It's almost all we know to do. And I think I'm being safe in that estimate. About 80%. We do use it, don't we? Well. We use it until we don't. We use it until we see something more interesting . . . until we see *game*.

Game! Game works better than shame.

But I'm jumping ahead. Let's stay with the discouraged people for a few seconds more to understand why that system doesn't get any results.

Let's look around and see what works in the real world of motivation. Let's watch a little league coach working with a young player.

We see that the player improves faster when the coach is supportive and building on small successes. See that? The coach is deliberately building the self-esteem and confidence of the player, little by little.

"Hey, Justin, that was *good!* Good swing. Now let's just level it out a little. Build on that good form you've got. And watch the ball all the way in. That's it! Way to go! Let's play a game of ten. I'll throw ten pitches and we'll see how many you can put a good swing on. See if you can beat your previous ten. See those guys over there in the stands? They're scouts, Justin! I think they're here from the Diamondbacks!"

Justin is trying not to smile. He is starting to love this

thing called baseball. He might just take some extra batting practice tonight.

Because encouragement and game-playing improve a player's performance. They're more efficient than yelling and criticizing. We see that all day long. Yelling doesn't build confidence. Players actually *lose* motivation when they are made to feel ashamed in front of their peers.

So with young athletes we use continuous and playful support. We make a game of it. But only because it works. If the other thing worked, we'd do it.

We can even see this at work in the training of animals. It's very effective motivation when a dolphin trainer gives a dolphin a small fish for jumping through a hoop. The dolphin *loves* that game. It's rewarding. It's a game! It's tapping into the happiness and fun and play and joy of the player—the dolphin—the living creature.

It would be destructive to punish the dolphin for not jumping through the hoop. Why would what is destructive in training animals work on people? How long would a shaming dolphin trainer keep his job? Screaming at his dolphin:

"Hey, you moron fish! Yeah, you! What the hell is it with all the leaping? You're missing the freaking hoop! What's the point of that? Where's your work ethic? Where's your pride? And what's with the grin? And that peeping noise!? You think this is funny? You think this is a game? Listen, entertainment is serious business. We put a lotta money in you."

I have got to remember that we are living creatures, too. We are like the dolphins. We are players in the great game of life. Why do we not understand that when we talk to ourselves? Why would something work on us that doesn't work on dolphins? Why do we just keep criticizing ourselves inside our minds? It can often begin right at the beginning of the day:

*Oh jeez, not another day. So much to dread. I can't believe I've left all those things unfinished. I know I'd have more energy if I went out for a run . . . or at least walked! But who has time when everything's so disorganized? I'm starting to envy my relatives who have passed away. I used to think I missed them, and that was depressing enough, but now I resent them and envy them, too. How come only **they** get to rest in peace? I didn't sleep well last night and that doesn't bode well for my challenges with procrastination. How will I ever process all my feelings around this? I should have gone to bed earlier.*

Am I willing to see how the "should haves" backfire? How they lower my mood and energy? The opposite of what I think I'm using them for. Do I fully understand how the shame shuts me down? Look at how I personalize everything unnecessarily. I see myself as *deserving* the criticism! Like I'm a prosecutor in a morals trial. Brought down by self-prosecution.

I can even make this failed system a part of my permanent identity. Now I believe it has to be solved in extremely subtle and nuanced ways over time. Perhaps I'll have to opt for ten to twelve years of expensive psychotherapy or some other form of spiritual cleansing.

The truth is it's merely a choice.

And that's such good news.

Because when I see that it's a choice that isn't working I don't have to make myself wrong or think it's caused by a permanent flaw. I don't have to add new chapters to my fabricated negative identity. I can simply ask myself, "Would another choice work better?" (Is there a game out there somewhere?)

And the answer to that is *yes.*

You can always get a game going.

Turning problems into games worked like a charm once I saw it and learned it. It also works for the clients I work with in my business. It works much better, much faster than shame. And it's more fun, which is not just some kind of icing on the cake or added benefit. Fun itself is the heart and soul of *why* it works.

We are drawn to things that are fun. We don't want to quit.

2

Motivation will no longer be necessary

We can actually become addicted after a while to things that are fun. If you have young people in your life you know how hard it is to pull them away from the games they are playing—the video games, the computer games, the games on their smart phone, the games in the driveway . . . because those games are fun.

Games do that for people.

Notice that a lethargic group of people sitting around in the living room thinking they are too tired to do anything but watch the Kardashians and eat doughnuts can come to life immediately when someone proposes that "we all play a game." It isn't long before everyone is laughing and shouting and having fun because they are now *playing*. This is the game element! If we really understand it and appreciate it, it will change our lives.

Once a game is joined, there's no need for me to also try to motivate myself. I am already tapped into that playful game energy. There's no whipping of the dolphin at this stage. The dolphin jumps freely from the joy of playing a game.

You can see on the internet that people are having fun

joining game groups when they want to accomplish something. There are groups on the internet who use pedometers and other devices to measure the exact number of steps they take each day. They do this for their health and for weight loss. But they really do this because it's play. They compete with other walkers. They keep score. It's a game now. The friendly competition produces energy and accountability. The fun of keeping score.

Contrast that to my saying to myself at the end of the day that *I should have exercised more. I should have taken a walk or two.* Or at the beginning of the day saying, *I should go to the gym today. I should get on the treadmill so I can trudge and trudge . . . I should do that.*

"Should" deflates and contracts.

Games inflate and expand.

Even the military understands the effectiveness of this choice. They play WAR GAMES because it's proven to be the best way for them to get ready.

Why aren't we taking more advantage of this marvelous, alternative choice? One big reason is that our culture thinks of games as frivolous. Non-productive. Not serious enough! But that's just way off the mark.

In my many years of coaching people (including coaching myself) games are the absolute best and most effective route to inspired action. They get me out of the stands and onto the field of play.

3

It's time to move your mouse

Our shaming thoughts are not original. We don't "create" them from some dark internal place as so many people like to believe.

We've picked these thoughts up from other people. They soon become the dialogue we can't get out of our heads, but they're borrowed. Many of us have grown up and hung out with other shame-based individuals, and so that's the language we learn.

This borrowing factor is good news when we can see it. We don't have to identify with these thoughts any more. We don't have to take them seriously. The jump (the shift, the choice) from a shame-based approach to a game-based approach then becomes as easy as shifting gears in a car, or moving your mouse to a better place to click.

4

Shouldn't I take this more seriously?

"I really have to do this," said Amanda in a low, sad voice.

We were talking about her new work project that was not getting off the ground. She was sad and scared.

"I'm so afraid of failure," she told me. "And I have a pattern of procrastinating and eventually giving up."

"What do you think the solution is?" I said (which is what a coach says when he himself doesn't have the solution).

"I need to be more committed," said Amanda. "I need to grow up. I need to take responsibility for my failure thus far and get more serious about the business."

"Sounds like fun," I said. And she could hear in my voice that I was only kidding.

"What do you mean by that?" she said.

"I mean it *doesn't* sound like fun."

"Well," she said, "it's not *supposed* to be fun, is it? It's work. That's why they call it work."

Amanda was trying to find a vein of shame to tap into. She thought she had let herself down, and if she became ashamed of herself—*really* ashamed of herself—she might force herself to succeed.

"There's no lightness in this," I said. "There's no way you're going to enjoy this."

"So you think positive psychology can paper over something real and serious?"

"No, I think you are at your best when you are having fun. And the only problem your business has had is your own lack of time and attention."

"I don't see the connection. I believe if I took it more *seriously*, I'd give it more time and attention."

"Well, no. I've never experienced that. Seriousness is stressful. By definition. Seriousness is not fun and addictive. Seriousness does not bring out the best in us. Games are addictive. They get our attention."

"Games!" she said. "This is not a game to me. I have bills to pay. I have a child to raise. This is no game."

"Precisely the problem," I said.

The Want-to vs. the How-to

Look, if you had, one shot, or one opportunity to
seize everything you ever wanted.
In one moment, would you
capture it, or just let it slip?

~ **Eminem**
Lose Yourself

1

A cure for intention deficit disorder

One day Amanda was practically weeping.

She was talking to me by phone and revealing her secret passion to me. (This call took place over eight years ago, a fact that will make this incident more understandable for you.)

"My secret hobby is to write screenplays and movie script ideas," she said. "I have a drawer full of them, and I'm just not sure what to do with them."

I asked her what she meant by that and she said she didn't know how to get them copyrighted or protected so no one would steal them, or so she'd have proper credit.

"How long has this been bothering you?" I said.

"It's been years. I just don't know how to interact with the whole world of copyrights or patents or whatever it is. It's so sad, too, a real shame, because some of them are such good ideas and they're just sitting in my drawer."

"Well," I said, "I think maybe this is your lucky day."

"Why? What? Do you know what to do? Do you know how to get a screenplay protected?"

"I do," I said.

And I heard this huge exhalation of joy on Amanda's end of the phone. Nirvana! It wasn't long before I was walking her through the steps she ought to take to get her ideas protected. She kept telling me to slow down so she could write down everything I was saying.

Finally she said, "You know what else I wish I knew how to do?"

"What's that?"

"How do I find agents or studios who might be interested in reading these?"

"You must have woken up on the right side of the bed today," I said.

"No!" she said. "You know that too?"

"I'll know it in about ten seconds," I said. "Because it hasn't come up on my screen yet . . . Oh, wait here it is: 'How to get your screenplay read in Hollywood.' You see, Amanda, I've been finding this on the internet while we were talking. I just Googled the exact questions you were asking, the things you said you didn't know how to do, and there they were. All these different blogs and articles. All these answers."

Amanda filled the silence that followed by feeling ashamed of herself . . . which was not my intention. I just wanted her to see that she was never really missing the how-to in the case of her screenwriting ideas. All she was lacking was an active, functional want-to.

But her momentary embarrassment would eventually go away as she woke up to a whole world of new opportunities for herself. She was now willing to see that most of the things in her life that she didn't think she knew *how to do* were just in need of an intention makeover.

2

You don't know how to do it?

When Sam Beckford and I wrote a book about small business owners and the lies they tell themselves, Lie #1 was about people saying they really just need to know *how* to succeed at their business.

They were fooling themselves.

And it's not just the business owners. We all seem to do this all the time.

We think we just need to know *how to* get clients, or we need to know *how to* increase cash flow or *how to* hire good people, or *how to* be happy, or *how to* communicate with our children, or *how to* lose weight. We think we don't know *how*! It is a self-deception that spills way across business boundaries and runs into personal life as well. It's a floodwater of self-deception.

Let me give you an example of this: If my teenage son is not cleaning his room it will never occur to me to go to him with a manual or a little e-book that teaches How to Clean Your Room. I know what's missing is not the how-to. What's missing is the want-to.

The want-to is almost always what's missing *whenever* something's not happening. It's not that we don't know how to do things. With the right level of desire, we can find that out very quickly.

Many people have come to me and said, "I *want to* be a public speaker. How do you start? I've wanted this so badly for a long time and I've never known *how to* do it!"

But the big missing piece here is, again, the want-to. Because achievement is about movement. It's not about rumination.

My unwelcome response is, "I don't really believe you want to be a speaker. Because if you wanted to, you would have already started. You would be out there speaking. *Some*where! So let's start with that realization. Then we can build from that truth. We can then start by strengthening your intention so that it moves you into action."

3

Will you take a carrot or a stick?

There are two thinking tools—two techniques—I use in my mind whenever I'm hung up on the how-to and I've left the want-to behind. I use them to strengthen my intention.

One way is the harsher, negative-motivation way, and that is asking myself, if I *had* to do this—if I *had* to sell a certain amount of product or if I *had* to raise a certain amount of money or if I *had* to have a great relationship with this person—what would I do? What steps would I take? What if someone put a handgun to my head and I had to do this to stay alive? I picture that. And then I start to brainstorm with myself. Soon I am furiously writing down the people I need to communicate with and the actions I need to take right now.

The other thinking tool is more positive. It also works for me. It goes like this: I imagine that someone just offered me a million dollars if I get this done. Will I accept the challenge?

Yes indeed.

If I knew that I would get a million dollars if I did this—this thing that I don't now even know *how to* do (I am thinking), this thing that I think is so hard and frustrating that I've been trying to start doing for a long time . . . Well—if I thought I was getting a million dollars for it, how would I approach it differently? What would I do differently right now?

These brainstorming games work. Because they kick me out of the how-to and put me in the middle of my strongest want-to.

4

It's hard to replace lost people

I remember once I had a client who sold home furnishings and furniture. He had a wonderful little team of about six saleswomen. But the company had a problem. They weren't good at recruiting and hiring salespeople. So whenever they lost a salesperson or two they would be short-handed. For a long time!

The owner, Monty, told me, "We have such a hard time finding good people. Is there anything you would suggest? Any techniques we don't know about?"

I told Monty he should have his own sales team give him people. Let *them* refer people in. I'd seen that work wonders for many of my other clients.

Monty said, "Oh, we've tried that. We've tried that and we've even offered to pay them a bonus if they bring someone on the team and that person stays here for six months and they perform at a certain level. We've offered them money! Still doesn't work."

I told him I thought it would work if someone really wanted it to work.

"Well," Monty said. "I think I just told you we tried it. I don't know if you were listening. We *did* want it to work. We just didn't know how to make it work. It's not that we don't want to. Maybe you're a little hung up on motivation as the answer to everything. For you it's the solution to everything, right? Well, maybe we just don't know how to do this."

I said, "Well, okay, but there's no right *way* to do it. It's about the *desire* to do it. I right now, personally, have a really huge desire to do this. Because I want to show you the difference between the how-to and the want-to. In other words, I really *want* your sales staff to bring people in and refer people to you. Is this making sense? And because this is something I really *want to* have happen, I'm going to show you that it *will happen* even though I don't know how right now. Just let me do it. I'll think of something."

And Monty looked at me. He said, "Well, all right, good luck. But don't spend any of my money. Or yours. Remember, we tried bonuses."

So one day I was in their showroom before store hours giving a brief sales workshop to their team. Their six women were sitting there in chairs listening to me. At the end of our time together I finished it up by saying, "I've given you all an index card. I'd like you each to write down two people in your world—two people you think might be good candidates to be on this team with you. They can be from your church, from your family, from a former business you worked at. They can be friends of yours. It doesn't matter where they're from, but write down the names of two people you think would be good teammates for you. These are people who you would really love to work with and who you think would succeed here if they were selling with you. And when you have your two names, bring the card up to me and then we can all leave. And thanks for doing this. Remember: just two names."

All six women sat there and wrote their names down. Some took longer than others, but they all did it. Now I had twelve prospects to join the sales staff. And it only took me about twenty minutes. So I went back to Monty and said, "I have twelve names here from your people. Referrals."

And he just stared at me. "How did you get them? Did you threaten them? How did that happen?"

I said, "We'll talk about that later," and I handed him the names.

He said, "Wait a minute. We don't have any contact information here."

I told him that was intentional. A good thing. Monty could now call each salesperson into his office one at a time and sit with her and talk to her about the two names he was given. He could ask them all about these people and take notes. He'd find out how to contact them once they briefed him on who they were and why they thought they'd be good. By doing this, Monty would know something about the prospects ahead of time. When he called them he could then start those relationships on the right foot.

Monty did all this! Reluctantly and joyfully—if that's possible. After eventually interviewing his twelve people he found six very good recruits. Pretty soon he even had a waiting list of people who wanted to work for their company. (He also got creative, feeling the energy from a renewed want-to, and devised other smart ways to bring in prospects.)

What was happening here?

This is it: When the mind goes to this want-to space, it tricks itself.

It tricks itself into clearing everything else out. Only the goal remains. So clean. So clear.

Agreement vs. Expectation

Fluctuations are aching in my soul.
Expectation is taking its toll.

~ Tame Impala
Expectation

1

Relationship problems can be solved

What solves our relationship problems with other human beings?

And what causes those problems to begin with?

I found the answers in a factory.

But I can apply those answers anywhere. To parenting, to a friendship—even to a love affair.

I was hired by a company that had performance and productivity breakdowns. I was asked to go train their people, to teach them higher levels of personal morale management and self-motivation. They hoped that maybe I could give them ways to do that, so that their people would wake up and take more ownership for their own attitudes. Get in here and help us, dude! Our factory workers aren't even recognizing their own self-defeating, victim thinking!

They were right. The people on the manufacturing line were not happy campers. Morale was low. But after a little asking around, I located the real problem. It wasn't the attitude of the line workers. It was the expectations of the leaders. Their leaders had lots of expectations. And they weren't aware of how toxic that approach was.

But how *could* they be aware of it? So very few people are.

For example, do you have expectations of someone in your life? How is that working out? I bet it's working as well as it was with the factory leaders.

Only two things can result from having expectations. One: the other person will not meet your expectation and you'll be disappointed (or even betrayed). Or, two: they *will* meet your expectation, and because you expected it, you won't feel *anything*, because, after all, it was what you expected. So your states of feeling will either be Disappointed or Nothing.

That's what expectations do for you. A life of swinging back and forth between feeling disappointed and feeling nothing at all. When I'm not disappointed, I'm feeling zero. Nada. Nothing.

In that company I was hired to train, the leaders had expectations of their people. They would walk around all day expecting things—they would expect certain levels of job performance, they would expect quotas to be reached, they would expect quality standards to be hit, and they would expect deadlines to be met. They would expect their expectations to be met—*met* like they *expected*!

The leaders talked to their people like this: "I expect you to ___. We expect you to ___. You're expected to ___." What did the workers think of that style of leadership? They thought it was:

Oppressive.

Weighty.

Heavy-handed.

Dispiriting.

Harsh.

Overbearing.

Dictatorial.

And so of course they were resenting all of it. They were saying that most of the expectations were unreasonable. The leaders didn't realize how understaffed they were, and therefore how stressed they were.

So the whole place was in a morale morass. A true crisis. The leaders were frustrated and upset and the workers were resentful and exhausted. Not a great combination.

One leader, Judd, couldn't believe his line foreman kept missing deadlines.

"We need better people," he told me. "People who have a sense of professionalism."

I asked Judd what his line foreman was doing wrong.

"He isn't delivering. I send him emails telling him what we need, and then when the customer comes to inspect the product it's not ready. Embarrassment all around."

I asked Judd what his agreement was with the foreman.

Judd gave me a strange look, as if I'd asked him what ballet step he was practicing this week. It was a look that said he just didn't see what I was getting at.

"Agreement?" he finally said.

"Yes," I said. "Agreement. What did you two agree to? What kind of agreement did the two of you make about the deadline and the product and the customer inspection?"

"He knew what he was supposed to do," said Judd.

And I noted that that was an expectation, not an agreement. I told Judd that in my experience, leadership by expectation was not effective, especially compared to leadership by agreement.

"Is this some kind of California thing?" Judd said.

He was ex-military and he ran his department by expectations, instructions and orders. And yes that might have worked somewhat in the army, but it was definitely not working for him now. His department was full of bad morale and near-mutiny.

It took me a while to convince Judd and the other leaders in that company to start leading by agreement and to drop the whole expectation thing. When they finally did, good results happened. As the months went by Judd would call me and grudgingly tell me about the many large and small successes.

He'd talk to his foreman and ask if the foreman would come sit down and co-create an agreement with him. He explained when the customer would be visiting and what products would need to be finished and ready to display during that visit.

Judd would say, "Can we have this ready by next Wednesday at ten?"

The foreman would say, "I'll try. We always give it our best shot. It won't be easy."

Judd knew that didn't constitute an agreement. It was just an honest response to a perceived expectation. So Judd did what he'd learned to do.

"What would it take for me to be able to count on the product being ready?" Judd asked the foreman.

The foreman said, "It's hard to say because we are short-handed right now."

Judd said, "Tell me what you need from me for us to have an agreement on this. What if I got you an extra person to work on your line between now and Wednesday?"

"That would definitely do it," the foreman said.

"Is that enough?" Judd said. "If I get you that you can make a commitment that I can count on?"

"Yes," said the foreman. And Judd reported that the deadlines were being met now. He said he was getting buy-in from the people on the line ahead of time, and that he was listening to their side of the story and giving them input into each agreement that got created.

Not only that, but in the rare instance that an agreement was not met, Judd was able to sit down with the other person and talk about where the agreement failed them. It wasn't personal anymore. It was only about the agreement. No longer any need to make anybody wrong. It was just an opportunity for a clearer and stronger agreement in the future.

Judd said, "One thing this system has done for me is that it's so much easier to have those difficult conversations when things do go wrong. In the past I was always gun-shy about confronting people and chewing them out. And they were always so defensive, nothing ever got solved. Now we don't have to talk about personal wrongdoing, we just talk about our agreements. How to make them more air-tight."

2

This can be a work of art

Agreements are creative by nature.

It's two people designing a work of art together. Therefore agreements are a lot more fun than expectations. Expectations are stressful. They lead to anxiety. I'll even say they are cowardly. Because my expectations allow me to put the blame for everything that goes wrong on other people. It's not me. It wasn't me. He didn't do what I expected! Really, I expected better from him.

But here's the good news: Expectations are not necessary. Oh, yes, they are rampant. Everybody seems to have them. But they are not necessary. In fact, it's actually possible to have no expectations of anyone, and to only have agreements when you need them.

3

A house built on shouting

I know a family who argued all the time. Their house was filled with shouting and name-calling. Sometimes "Screw you!!" was all you'd hear on an otherwise sunny Saturday morning. One daughter kept quoting Amy Winehouse by yelling, "What is this fuckery?"

So I met with the father, Stewart, to see if we could sort this out.

"Maybe you could create an agreement," I said. "All of you, together, when the mood is relaxed and happy, maybe sitting around a friendly table together."

Stewart was skeptical. He said this shouting thing ran deep in his family history. His parents used to throw plates and stuff.

"It runs deep," he said.

"We respond to fleeting, ethereal, negative thoughts," I said, trying to sound like I was from India. "Nothing runs 'deep.' That's a myth. That's a geological metaphor that doesn't apply. You're not a planet. You won't understand your mind or your family by thinking that way."

Stewart was listening. But he was not understanding. Do

you blame him?

So I decided to take a different tack. I decided to shift from India to Little Italy in New York. I asked him if his family ever ordered pizza.

"Yes."

"When the pizza delivery boy or man comes to the door, how do you treat him?"

Stewart said he wasn't sure if he understood my question. He said, "We're nice to him."

I asked if they were *extremely* nice to him, if they smiled at him, joked with him about the weather, and called out a cheerful, "Thank you!" and "Take care!" and "Have a great evening!" and Stewart said yes, all of those things.

I said, "Do you always do this, no matter who the delivery person is?"

"Yes, I guess so."

"And when you have your box of pizza in your hand, do you then return to your bickering, hostile family and start the arguments back up?"

"A lot of the time, yes."

"So you're all treating some unknown person far better than you are treating yourselves, your family—the people you love the most."

Stewart nodded his head. I asked him if he were willing to lead a family meeting in which they all agreed to communicate with each other with a baseline of kindness and courtesy—the same level of kindness they find *so easy* to give the delivery boy.

"We could try that," he said, "but it will be hard. At least at the beginning."

"You'd be going against family tradition," I said.

"Right!"

I asked him if it would ever occur to him to open the door when the pizza delivery boy arrived and yell at him, "Damn you! You *never* listen to me. You'll never change, you selfish a**hole! Screw you!!!!"

Stewart stared at me without any expression. We both knew I was being a little strange, but I wanted to do that to make this insight work for him.

"I have another idea," I said, "in case the family meeting doesn't produce an agreement."

"What is that?"

"You could go to Domino's and buy one of their uniforms and hats, and the next time some family member starts arguing with you, you can go into your room and put the uniform on and re-emerge. I think when they saw you in that pizza uniform they would treat you really differently. Maybe your whole family could get fitted for them."

4

What have we fallen into?

One young woman told me she yelled at her husband and called him all kinds of humiliating names because that's what her mother did to her father. She thought it might even be "healthy" to vent that way and then try to have "make-up sex" and make it an even better relationship in the long run.

"And," I said, "does it work?"

She said she was surprised that it was *not* working out.

"How did it work for your mom and dad?"

"They got divorced."

"What am I missing? I can be slow at times."

As we talked on she became hopeful and excited when she learned there was a choice available to her between expectations and agreements. And that agreements could be what she and her husband could use to feel better about each other. And that they might work even better than "healthy, vulnerable, transparent venting."

5

Expectations weigh a lot

Amanda wondered whether she was willing to look at how many expectations she had of other people (with an eye to dropping them).

"How do I find out what my expectations are?" she said.

I asked her to make a list of her disappointments. That would do it. Who was she disappointed with? What are some of the behaviors of other people recently that left her feeling let down or upset? She had a good, long list after thinking about it.

Because expectations lead to disappointment, you can trace it backwards from disappointment to expectation. Any disappointment she had in life would not have been there if she had no expectation.

"I'm disappointed when my husband doesn't volunteer to clean the dishes after I have made a dinner for us," she said. "It's like he doesn't get the work I've done. Or else he thinks I should be doing all this dinner stuff and be cleaning up afterward as well."

I said, "Is there a gentle request that you could make?"

Amanda thought for a while and then said, "Maybe."

"What might you say to him? Something that could encourage a new agreement."

Amanda said, "I could say, 'Hey, Jason, would it kill you to participate a little bit in our evening here?'"

"Okay. Maybe something even warmer than that."

"'Jason, dude, could you stand to step outside of a world that's all about you, all Jason, all the time, and show a brief gesture of partnership? Might you just do the mother-loving dishes? You can return to your inner world right after. I'll go downstairs to call my girlfriend. I won't bother your introspection any further after that. I'll even sleep in a different room if that will help you hold your focus on yourself.'"

I nodded my head. "Okay, that's a beginning."

Amanda looked pleased with herself and a little more relaxed. Then she said, "You know, I think he's actually just innocent in this."

I waited for her to continue. She was seeing something important. Then she said, "He's just a little clueless, you know? I guess I could say, 'Could we have an agreement? I have an idea for one, but only if you agree.' And then I could ask if he'd participate. The more I think about it, the more I think he'd gladly do it if I put it that way."

6

I want to hear your complaints

Sometimes I am hired to mediate disputes between business partners. When I sit down with the two partners (I will disguise their true identities by calling them Punch and Judy), the first thing I want to hear are the complaints.

When Punch lists the complaints he has about Judy, we are off to a good start. Because complaints can always be converted into requests. And requests can be converted into agreements.

The three of us, Punch, Judy and me, were sitting around a table in a small hotel conference room. The conversation went this way:

PUNCH: Judy keeps me in the dark about her activities and the customers she's negotiating with.

ME: Okay. Is there a request you'd like to make of Judy?

PUNCH: If she met with me once a week so we could just go over what she's doing, and what I'm doing, I wouldn't feel like I was in the dark all the time. I also wouldn't be contacting people she's already contacted.

ME: Judy, would that be doable for you? One regularly scheduled meeting with Punch each week to go over everything?

JUDY: Yes, I could do that. Punch doesn't remember this but I suggested that a year ago when we were just getting started and he said he didn't think it was necessary, that we could just stay in touch instead.

PUNCH: You're right. I was wrong. I never anticipated how busy things would get.

ME: Do we have an agreement?

They both chose a day and time for their weekly meeting.

Complaints are toxic when they aren't converted into requests. They soon turn into resentments. And it isn't long before those resentments show up to the party dressed as irreconcilable differences.

But when they are seen as good ways to start a meeting, then we can have a very creative meeting ending up with agreements.

7

But what if we are not saints?

A lot of people think, "If I have negative feelings, if I'm judging someone critically, if I'm upset with someone, it's *healthy* to say it. It's *healthy* to attack, it's *healthy* to hurt someone else, because that takes the hurt out of *me*."

Now how sensible is that, really?

I had a client who said he had a fight with his wife and I asked him, "How was it?" and he said, "Well, you know what that's like. You've had those."

And I said, "No, I really haven't."

And he said, "Oh, come on."

I said, "I really haven't. Kathy and I have been together for over twenty-five years, and we've never had a real fight."

He said, "Well . . . I . . . Oh, yeah, okay . . . I forgot that you're a saint, right? But I'm not. I'm a regular person."

I said, "No, no, it's not that, I'm not a saint at all. In fact if you look at my biography, I probably shouldn't be allowed to walk the earth a free man. So I'm not a saint, but I'll tell you that I don't fight with her, and it's for the same reason that I don't punch the mailman when he's late, or I don't strangle that cat in my backyard and kill it. Same reason exactly—I just don't want to. I've decided it's not the kind of behavior I want to indulge in. I won't do it. I just won't do it. It's not useful."

You hear so many people say, "Oh, fights are great, aren't they? They clear the air, they purge things, they're so wonderful."

The only people I've ever heard say that are now divorced people. Because, no, they are not wonderful. They're hurtful. They're unforgettably hurtful, and they're mean and they're demeaning and every fight is just bitterly selfish. It's like two children scratching each other's eyes out. When little children do that you separate them immediately. You put them in different rooms and explain that we humans don't do that to each other.

But when grown-ups do it? Oh, how therapeutic! How wonderful! How authentic we are! How transparent and vulnerable!

Expectations are what lead to fights, arguments and negative judgments of another human being. If we have no expectations, only agreements, fights don't have to occur.

8

Learning from the
Godfather movies

There's a problem with the very word, expectation. How do you feel when you hear it? How do you feel in your gut when someone walks in and says, "Here's what I *expect* of you."

Rebellion? That's what I feel. I feel my inner spirit rise up. No one likes to have expectations placed on them by other humans. It gives the expector false superiority. I don't accept that superiority. In fact, down deep, we all realize that none of us were put here on earth to live up to the expectations of other people.

So that's why expectations don't work. But why do agreements work so much better?

There's a funny thing about human beings. Human beings do not like breaking their word. And I mean all human beings, including criminals. They don't like it. You follow the *Godfather* movies, *The Sopranos*, you know the oath, you know honor among thieves as a concept. That's very real. That wasn't made up for the movies. People will do a lot to keep their word. People will not live up to your expectations—in fact most people will *try* to *not* live up to your expectations—but they *will* try to keep their word.

9

Are you a person of interest?

Why is it, that when a married woman is found dead, the spouse is the first person law enforcement looks at as a person of interest? Shouldn't the spouse be the *last* person we suspect?

This is all because of expectations.

10

Life as an unexpected pleasure

It's running into someone *unexpectedly* that is the most fun in life.

"What an unexpected pleasure!" people say. Can we hear them when they say that? Are we really listening? What. An. Unexpected. Pleasure. There's no pleasure like it.

What an unexpected pleasure *life* is to a child!

And then, in that child's life, expectations start to accumulate, and life gets to be less of a pleasure. That's the process by which stress and pain accumulate after childhood. It's not circumstances, it's expectations. We are so worried about the thoughts and actions of other people! We expect better from them.

People are put on this planet to amuse us. *Not* to live up to our expectations. They have no other purpose than to be amusing and lovable. When we realize that, we can stop worrying about them.

11

He will not be at your wedding

When he was a young man, Alan Watts used to be a minister, and he would perform marriage ceremonies. When he met with the couple before the ceremony, he would say, "You know, I have only one question for you that would disqualify me from being the person who officiates at this marriage ceremony. I have one question of you as a couple and that is this. If either one of you expects the other to change in some fundamental way after you are married, I will not perform the ceremony because your marriage won't work. I will not bless it."

Very wise man, Alan Watts.

12

Life beyond just good enough

Yes, I hear you. You think this is humanly impossible. Your husband and you have some real problems. You worry about him. It's frustrating. But what if . . . What if your only job was to love him? How would that simplify your life? You could have a life with no expectations of him whatsoever.

It is possible, and I've worked with people who have learned to do it—to go home, and walk into the home, and have absolutely no expectations whatsoever of any person in that home.

That feels so good. It feels so light-hearted and free. It's so much easier to love someone when you are feeling that.

ELEVENTH CHOICE

Testing vs. Trusting

What about that millionaire
with the drumsticks in his pants?
He looked so baffled and so bewildered
when he played and we didn't dance.

~ **Bob Dylan**
Don't Fall Apart On Me Tonight

1

This is what stops us

This is how most people stop themselves.

They tell themselves things like, "I don't believe it would work." "I don't have enough desire for it." "I don't have enough passion." "I don't trust it yet." "I guess I have to be more of a believer before I start doing this."

And so they are all hung up on these very deep emotional ideas. Darkly sentimental deficits are soon showing up in waves. Not believing in yourself, not believing in a process, not trusting this, wishing for that, hoping, seeking confidence . . . All the fearful, gothic and romantic concepts that stop us. We believe they are necessary.

"I guess I really have to believe in myself more in order to move forward and be good at this job. I guess . . ."

Well, no. Not really. I mean, hey. You can relax.

In fact, if I'm coaching you, I want you to cross all that stuff off your list. You know that list you have? Of things your thought-life is missing? Like belief in yourself? Like the willingness to trust things? You make the list because you think you have to trust something before you do it. You don't. I want you to cross off "believe in myself" as something you need to do today.

Once you cross that off you can see how simple your day has become. You no longer have to trust something before you do it. Now all you're going to do is do it.

2

Did you think walking would work?

When you were a little baby, you didn't have to *trust* that walking would work. You didn't have to believe in yourself or have specific faith that you would learn to walk like grown-ups walk.

And so you stumbled around, and you fell, and you giggled, and you fell, and you cried. But then you got back up and you stumbled a while more and finally, days later, you were walking.

There wasn't really a trust in there that you had to master first. There was only your innate willingness to *test*. The human gift for adventure. (That we eventually talk ourselves out of.)

Now as you got a little older you saw that your friends in the neighborhood were riding bikes. And your brother and sister had a bike and they rode theirs. And it seemed like everybody had a bike. But the more you looked at a bicycle the more you saw that it didn't really seem to make sense that these two wheels would hold you up. It sure looked like you would just tip over if you got on the bike. And so you got up on the bike and it tipped over and you fell.

But somehow you knew that you didn't have to trust that

the bicycle would hold you up in order to learn to ride it. All you had to do was be willing to keep testing it.

I know when I learned how to ride a bike I didn't trust it at all. So my mind's internal mantra was, "This will never work. This will never work!! I don't see how this could work. Oh, it might work for others—but I don't think it will work for me."

But then, after I fell, I got back up on the bike. I kept doing that. Soon I was riding the bike.

But I was young. I was not a grown-up yet. A grown-up in a similar situation, with a similar thing they are trying to learn how to do, gets on the bike, falls off the bike, and then sues the bike company.

Then they join a support group with other people who have fallen off *their* bikes. And they meet in the old church basement every Wednesday night and share their stories about what victims they are and how horrible it was to get their hopes up about riding a bike, and all they did was fall off when they tried it.

That's what grown-ups do. Living in a world that is so hard to trust.

Failure is embarrassing and something you should never put yourself in a position to experience, right? Not if you're a grown-up. You shouldn't expose yourself to public failure for any reason ever—so, therefore, be careful, don't even *try* to ride a bike until you can believe that it will work.

Meanwhile the child (their mind clear of sentiment and fear) is yelling, "Look, Ma, no hands!" Because this first time around the block on a bike?

Well . . . it's just crazy good.

3

There are people in the water

Oh, look. There are people in the water, swimming. It looks fun.

I'd love to learn how to do that, but you know what? When I put a big stone in the water it goes right to the bottom, and I weigh a lot more than the stone. So if you ask me if I trust that the water will hold me up? No, I don't. In fact, I don't believe it will hold me at all. I don't see how it *could*.

Here, let me show you. Here's a stone. OK? It might weigh as much as five pounds. We put it in the water and it goes right to the bottom and dies. Now how can I, who weigh so much more than the stone, get in the water without sinking to the bottom? (And dying. Unless somebody pulls me out. Real fast.) This is frightening.

Now here's what eventually happens: sometimes with the help of a swimming teacher, sometimes with the help of floaties, sometimes with the help of this or that, I start to *test* this thing called swimming. And I try it and I test it and I test it and I try it and after a while it *works* for me!

It works because of my willingness to test, test, test, and try. It doesn't work because I figured out how to trust it or because I learned how to believe in myself or because I learned how to believe in the water, or I learned how to believe in the universe that made the water.

I notice that I've never heard a child say, "My life isn't working for me." I mean, that might show up in a funny *Peanuts* cartoon. We would all laugh at the grown-up words spoken by the little kid. But a real child doesn't think that way. That child is too busy experimenting.

4

Wanting trust instead of a life

I'll give you another example. You don't need to be a coach to appreciate this example. I have a coaching school that isn't there to teach you how to be a coach but how to have a prosperous practice and be a creative business owner and get clients. And inside the school we have systems and methods for getting clients.

Yet, some people prior to coming to the school read up on these systems and they say to me, "I guess I'm just going to have to trust that this school will work for me."

And I say, "You know, you don't. I'll tell you what the experience is of people who have been to the school. Those who practice (test) the disciplines in the school succeed, and you can come practice and test them yourself or you can come bite your nails and observe everyone else and wonder if this will work for you."

Well, that's too testy. Maybe I won't say it like that. At least not in the future.

But still. Some people want to be like people going to a gym, pulling up a lawn chair and watching everyone working out. They are watching people swim, watching people on the machines and just observing. They wonder if it will work for them. They see such strong, slim, fit bodies, but still they don't know if they should trust it.

They don't understand that it is the *action* that moves people forward. And trusting has no place in it. And this is such good news. It takes many heavy challenges off your mind.

5

Life as a series of experiments

Testing means experimenting, and as the brilliant business author Dale Dauten says, "Experiments never fail."

Experiments never fail because when you are experimenting you are just as eager to find out what *doesn't* work as what does. Whatever you find out helps you grow. There is no failure in that.

Experiments give you a way to play with the universe. They allow you to interact with the real world and get some interesting answers. What works? What doesn't? Let me try again. This is starting to energize me.

TWELFTH CHOICE

Purpose vs. Personality

All through the day:
I me mine I me mine I me mine.

~ **George Harrison**
I Me Mine

1

When I need to get into the kitchen

I am all possibilities.

I am brought to life by purpose.

If I have a purpose to go to the kitchen and get some kale juice (and by that I mean a chocolate milkshake), the purpose takes me there. My personality does not.

Today when Amanda says, "I have a pattern of . . ." I stop and say, "Yes, okay, but that's in the past. What would you like to do *now*, today? What would you like to *choose* to do?"

That would shift her to a chosen purpose.

One day Amanda was looking hopeful but still a little skeptical.

She said, "Okay. I'm always late, I have a pattern of being late, I show up late for meetings . . ."

Her personality. Her identity. She's a thing. A fixed entity. An *it*. *It* shows up late. It always does.

I said, "In the past there were meetings you showed up late for. I understand that. Those are unimportant facts about the past. Today you have a meeting at three p.m., right? What would you like to choose to do?"

"Well, I have a pattern of being late. My personality is . . . I'm disorganized."

"Well, yes, and you're making that up right now. You're creating that story right now as you think it and speak it. You're coming to me out of thin air! What would you like to choose to do for this meeting, today? Would you like to be on time?"

"Yes, I'd like to . . . But I'm worried that, well, you know, given who I am, that's just the way I am."

She was so enmeshed and bought-in to all these permanent characteristics of hers that she couldn't yet see the freedom of choice that is always there. She couldn't see that she could base her actions on her purpose, not her personality. Therefore, she had no way to tap in to her own unlimited creative power.

But it would be beautiful when she saw that she could.

2

It's what's beneath my wings

When there's a purpose, everything changes.

I'm tired and my mind is fading as I am finishing a long drive into L.A., but I suddenly realize I don't have all that much further to go.

There is a nice hotel and soft bed waiting for me, and I see on the screen that I'm only ninety-nine miles from L.A. and hey, that's good and that's uplifting and that's my purpose kicking in! I'm about to get there! Purpose gives me surprising energy. It is my second wind.

3

It was like me and John Belushi

When I was in my senior year at college I was all ready to graduate when my counselor called me in to tell me I was three units shy in my minor. I would have to take a class in the summer to make that up and then graduate many months later.

That was not okay with me.

I was tired from many long nights studying for finals, but now I had a new purpose: find some way to graduate on time!

It had been *twelve years* since I started college! I felt like John Belushi in *Animal House*. Oh no! Twelve years of college down the drain!

Most people graduate in four years, and even though some of my years were taken up by time in the army, twelve years to graduate was embarrassing. Of course, it wasn't really a mystery. My college life had been a life of no purpose. I was drunk and partying and writing songs and poetry, but that was all to distract me from the fact that I had no life purpose and had become an alcoholic.

So now I wanted to graduate. Finally! Could I at least have that?

So I started calling my professors to see if any of them would help me do this. Finally I found one who said he would give me my three extra units of credit if I wrote a very long research paper and got a good grade on it. I talked to my counselor and she said the University of Arizona would accept the units if the professor submitted them within the week. One week!

So day and night I studied and typed and typed. I was not tired. I had huge energy! Even though nothing had changed physically. I didn't get extra sleep or drugs or anything other than a purpose. I submitted the paper, the professor approved it, and I graduated on time.

It was not "like me" to do this. My personality was not like that. But fortunately I didn't go there.

4

All we are is dust in the wind

I was not a purpose-driven person growing up. (For me, growing up took about fifty-five years. That's normal, right?)

I walked around with this idea that I was programmed and coded by this thing called my personality to be a certain way. A way that left purpose out of the equation. (And how convenient it was to be run by a robotic program instead of making choices. Robotically living the almost-good-enough life and not even seeing that I could have a crazy-good life if I'd known about the choices.)

Permanent personality, for me, was such a no-brainer. Doesn't it seem obvious? And simple! I believe I have a permanent personality and then *allow it to run me!* Sure I was suffering, but who wasn't? (Nathaniel Branden once said to me, "Suffering is the easiest way to live.")

The underlying, hidden problem with my approach to life was that the central premise of my life was not true. It was an illusion. This thing called personality is *not* permanent. It's an illusion that it's permanent. It's an illusion that it even exists. It's just a collection of opinions, memories, fears and judgments. Swirling in and swirling out. Like dust in the wind. And until we know about this choice, this dust called personality is *all we are.*

5

Today I question every thought

Today I question every thought that arises about my so-called personality.

And the most fun part of doing that is that I get to invent all day. Like I knew to do when I was three years old. Before I got talked out of it! (By myself and others.)

When Ralph Waldo Emerson saw that we were being talked out of our natural playful selves he said, "Society everywhere is a conspiracy against the manhood of every one of its members."

(Today he would have said ". . . a conspiracy against the personhood of each of its members," but you get his point.)

Most people in adulthood have dropped invention out of their activity. They don't invent. But if they could set aside the illusions that they have bought into about their "personality," then all of a sudden what would be left?

Pure creativity.

6

But I saw it on Dr. Phil

Someone told me the other day that Dr. Phil says that "the best predictor of future behavior is past behavior."

I like Dr. Phil. I think Dr. Phil has really done a lot of good in the world because of how he challenges people. But I do not agree with him that the best predictor of future behavior is past behavior.

My experience is that the best predictor of future behavior is *current choice.*

Phil thinks the past creates the present. But the truth is, and I will repeat this so that I myself can remember it, **the present creates the past.**

Look how we've got it completely backwards. We've got it reversed in our minds. This is where the whole illusion of causative personality begins. It comes from this. This exaggerated, kneeling down, bowing down to the past as the source of all actions in the present. It's not. The past is simply the past. We call it the past because it has passed. It has even passed away. It has kicked the bucket. It's over and gone.

Memories from my past (even though you could conceivably draw an artistic, nebulous pattern out of them, just as you can see animals in the clouds) are not an *active* pattern that motivates me. These memories are simply interesting (if often inaccurate) flurries of faded information. Actually, they are not even interesting unless I pretend they are.

7

It's clouds' illusions I recall

When we are young we are given a name. That name is usually fairly arbitrary and always just dreamed up by our parents. But soon we cover our name with stories about who we really are. We believe we are becoming significant.

If somebody says to me when I am young, "You're never on time. You're always running late. You never plan ahead!" I just believe that automatically. Why wouldn't they know the truth? OK. That's me. That's significant. That's part of who I am! Instead of realizing *I made a choice that had me show up late.* I don't see that. I immediately see a pattern emerging from my identity.

It's obvious, looking back, that personality traits are just randomly thrown at us. Like paints thrown on a canvas at random. We could have all been named Jackson Pollock. The paint spots and splatter could be from the words of a father, or a sibling who says one thing, my best friend or a teacher who shouts something at me when I am young (about *me*), and all of a sudden I am gazing at a multi-colored canvas called my permanent-personality-art-museum self.

No wonder we go out into the world unaware of our choices!

No wonder we're always scared of who we are, and

worried about whether we have the capability to do the things we think other people are doing so easily because of who *they* are.

The truth is better than all that.

The truth is we can be whoever we choose to be in any given moment. That's all we do anyway, we just don't see it. We don't have to be who we think we already permanently are. Look at all the nervous energy it takes to hold that illusory, multiple mosaic of a person together all day!

A second-century Indian scholar named Aryadeva, writing 1,900 years ago, said, "Could it be that this highly-knit sense of self is not what it seems? Do we really need to hold everything together, and *can we*? Is there life beyond self-importance?"

Transformation vs. Information

Inch by inch, row by row,
I'm gonna make this garden grow,
all it takes is a rake and a hoe,
and a piece of fertile ground.

~ David Mallett
The Garden Song

1

My life was stuck in the mud

What happens if I have a choice but I don't know it? What if I don't see it?

Now that's the most interesting part (I believe) about these choices and about the very real possibility of living a crazy-good life.

In my life (looking back over the years) I was really *stuck*. I didn't know I had a choice to become unstuck. Like a car is stuck in the mud, I was stuck in so many categories, and for more years than most of you have been alive.

Now that's a pretty sad thing, because I didn't *need* to be stuck. I just didn't see the choices.

Sometimes it starts with knowing the difference between information and transformation.

Let me give you an example of this choice. With this example, I'm going to sound like I'm mean and uncaring and stereotyping. But I'll do it anyway, even exaggerate it a little bit, to make a point.

When I give seminars these days I notice some people when they first come into the room. They sit down and they are looking up to the front of the room, and I can almost see it in their eyes—they are here for information only.

They have that edgy look in their eyes. Impatient. Wondering if they should really be somewhere else. One last double-thumbing of the smart phone. Now they look pensive. Did they leave the oven on at home? Will they return to a whirlwind of smoke and ashes? Is this seminar a waste of time? Don't I already know this stuff?

These are the information people. It's in their eyes. They walk the earth like info-zombies. Life to them is only about knowing stuff.

But let's look and see: who else is in the room?

Oh, yes, there they are: the transformation people!

The transformation people look different. Their eyes are sparkling with a look of quiet excitement. They laugh with the person sitting next to them. They have one of my books under their chair and I notice it has a multitude of little colored stickers coming out of the pages, some pale blue, some pale yellow and some pink. Oh my. They are already *using* this stuff!

These are the people who are the most fun to teach.

2

Transformation means change

Transformation simply means change—my life is going to *change* out of what I get today. I am going to *apply* what I learn. I'm going to experiment with what I've learned today. I am going to listen all day with *usefulness* in mind. How can I use this?

Meanwhile, the information people are listening for whether they agree with the information. Then they debate with themselves about whether they already "knew it."

Those who are here for information will tell you, "Man, I've been going to seminars for years, I go to all these self-help programs, I've signed up for this, I did Tony Robbins years ago, I did the fire walk, I did that, I did positivity training and took a year-long course in spiritual vulnerability, and still nothing changes. Once I did a weekend in Sedona learning inner personality types and I found out I was an introvert, which I never knew, and it was disheartening. I withdrew for awhile. I hope this information is new."

Transformation people don't have to hope the information is new. To them, everything is new.

3

This can make your life a joke

Now you're in my course on learning to make money. I am teaching you that learning to make money is just like playing the piano.

It's the same process.

If you want to make more money, you will step into transformation and test the outer edges of whatever you do to make money now.

If I want to learn to play the piano, I won't just read books *about* the piano. I won't just watch videos of people showing me how to play the piano. Because I could do that for years, and people might challenge me to actually *play*!

"All this information you have, show us. Show us what you can do with it."

And I would sit at the piano and, of course, there wouldn't be anything I could do with it—nothing at all. The audience would grow restless. I'd try to make a joke. Turn the theme of the evening from music to comedy.

That's information for you. It can make your life a joke.

So why do I pursue it?

I keep thinking it will show me *how to* do things.

But that's the problem with information. It pushes you into a how-to world. It's a lost world. You're starring in *Lost*. Its inhabitants are all the people who don't know *how* to do what they *want* to do. Or so they think.

You can read a lot of books on piano playing. Or on *how to* ride a bicycle. You can go to a seminar on bicycle riding, and you can get all the information in the world. You can even read Lance Armstrong on how to ride a bicycle (with or without supplements). But if you are not out there experimenting with riding the bicycle, you won't be able to ride a bicycle.

But wait. There's good news in all of this.

4

I challenge you to grab this

I'll give you the example of someone I will call Travis. Travis is a very prosperous, very successful life coach right now and he wasn't a few years ago. He really wasn't.

He read a lot of books before he came to one of my coaching prosperity schools and I could see it in his eyes that he wanted something that he could *use*. He didn't simply want more information. I admired his questions and his participation and the way he pulled actionable insights from the course. He was always looking for what he needed to take out into the world and apply and test and experiment with. And every month he made his reports to me, and his income went up, up, up, up. People would turn to him and say, *Tell me how to do it! What are you doing that I'm not doing?*

He said, "I don't know. Really? I am just doing."

What he was doing that they weren't doing was called doing!

They wrote it down. (*They wrote it down!*)

He said to them, "You are just absorbing and accumulating concepts—learning, learning, learning. I challenge you to take it, grab it, run out there and work with it. You want to see for yourself that you can *use* it!"

5

A great leap forward
is what stops us

One book I have been reading (and I'm on my second time through it) is by Matt Furey. I say I'm on my second time through because some of my friends have made up a slogan: "Once for information, twice for transformation."

What they mean is that any book you read just once adds more information to the brain. But when you read it twice it lands in a deeper place, and has a real shot at leading you into new action.

Matt Furey's book is called *Expect to Win - Hate to Lose.* He has a chapter in it called "Your Great Leap Forward," and that's meant to be ironic. Because what the chapter is really about is *not* taking a great leap forward. His point is that the whole idea of a great leap forward is exactly what stops us! That desire to make some quantum Knievel jump across the canyon from failure to success. And then being scared to do it. And then, eventually, *trying* the big leap and failing. All the while not understanding that transformation can occur beautifully with tiny, tiny steps.

Matt quotes John Wooden, the great UCLA coach who had more national championship basketball teams than any other coach. And here's what John Wooden says:

> "When you improve a little each day, eventually big things occur. When you improve conditioning a little each day, eventually you have a big improvement in conditioning. Not tomorrow, not the next day, but eventually a big gain is made. Don't look for the big quick improvement, seek the small improvement one day at a time. That's the only way it happens and when it happens, it lasts."

He is recommending *small* improvements each day.

Let's look again at the example of me coming up in front of the room to play the piano. What if I had mixed in, with all that information from piano books I read, piano seminars I went to, something very small—a practice—let's say ten minutes a day on the piano? What if I'd sat at the piano for ten minutes to go through the exercises the book recommended? And then just fooled around with the keys after. Just ten minutes. That's it. That's all I did. But every day.

What would happen over time?

My experience is that the results can be quite fun.

6

Fifteen minutes and then you can bail

Sometimes my clients who are writing books tell me, "I'm stuck! I'm stuck and I just bought three books on How to Write Your Book! I've been reading these books, so why haven't I made any progress on my own book? I've got to finish reading these books because they're giving me wonderful information about how to write a book."

But no book. No real writing. Just wonderful information!

Nassim Taleb says, "To bankrupt a fool, give him information." To bankrupt an author, same thing. Tell her she doesn't have enough know-how yet.

When I'm coaching authors I might ask them to accept my challenge: fifteen minutes a day on your book. You don't have to write anything great, just darken the page. That's all you have to do. Start with the blank pages, and darken them. Just do it. Fifteen minutes and then bail on yourself. You can go longer if you're loving it, but never shorter.

And again it sounds kind of silly, but so many people that I work with don't know they have a choice to transform. What they tell me is that they are dumbfounded and disheartened by all the information they have taken in on the subject and by their total lack of progress in the real world.

They're pretty downhearted, but what are they now looking for? Are they now looking for what's wrong with their premise? Where their system is broken? No. They're looking for *more information*—better information.

And they call me and say, "Hey, I just found out about a new guy who teaches how to do this in a radical new way—I think I'm signing up for his course!"

That's just more information.

If you write fifteen minutes a day, radical changes occur in the world. Creation happens. Whether you want it to or not. Once you open yourself to that channel, productivity happens, and there's nothing you can do to prevent it.

7

Afraid to leave my safe house

I was once so accustomed to my comfort zone that I built up a form of agoraphobia—fear of leaving home (home being my comfort zone). Home was where I was thinking I was safe.

I was not *comfortable* writing a song or a talk or a book. I didn't know how to make it great, I didn't know how to make it perfect, I didn't even know how to make it good. I was not comfortable writing anything yet. I thought I wasn't inspired. But in truth, I just wasn't comfortable.

I was also not comfortable playing the piano. What if someone hears me? Are you kidding? A grown man playing *Heart and Soul* or *Twinkle, Twinkle Little Star*? I didn't know if I should use a teacher or study online or learn to read music first.

And so the problem in my life was always that there was nothing going on that would change that mindset. Until there was.

And then everything opened up, and out flew these choices.

8

A ridiculously small amount of time

Are you now thinking that ten or fifteen minutes a day is a foolishly small amount of time? Are you thinking that I am lost in this pipe dream?

Then I'll raise the ante on you.

Are you ready to get absurd?

Listen to what Matt Furey says:

"If you don't think you have enough time to clean your home or office, then commit to cleaning it for one minute. Get started and see if you can stop in one minute—I bet you can't. How much could you improve your life if you took a small step each day on something you have been putting off? How much could you change your life if you did the following each day:

One minute of exercise.

One minute of deep breathing.

One minute of cleaning.

One minute to learn a new word or phrase.

Smiled and said hello to one person.

Read for 1 minute."

This is what Matt Furey writes, and Matt Furey was a world champion martial artist, a national champion wrestler, really prosperous internet guru, really prosperous health and exercise guru, author, teacher, seminar leader. And he recommends one minute. One minute!

Now, why? That sounds kind of silly. Why one minute? How would that change the way I live my life?

Even one minute outside your comfort zone is powerful because it stretches you. It opens you. It grows you. You are now in *action*.

Finally it dawned on me: the only real problem here is my comfort zone.

I now see that all growth takes place *outside* my comfort zone. And that's exactly where I never go! In fact, it was my life's unconscious mission and my personal internal commitment to never leave my comfort zone. To never embarrass myself. To never go beyond. (*Good* was an okay goal but *crazy good* was only for weird, courageous geniuses like Amelia Earhart, Steve Jobs or The Beatles.)

I was living a life of avoidance. I wasn't growing in creativity or courage. I was avoiding the very thing that would make me the happiest: small transformative steps and actions. Outside my comfort zone.

Finally in my late forties I got it back. That thing I had when I was three. The fun and the daring. I got coaching from someone who wouldn't let me stay at home. (You can Google my coach, Steve Hardison, known worldwide as the ultimate coach.) And soon things were going well, and then from going well to . . . well . . . you know where.

9

Taking that small, embarrassing step

Children learn to ride a bike by twisting and falling and jumping back up on the bike. They fall off, they get back on. "Oweeee, my knee is bruised and bleeding! But hey . . . this is also fun!"

Children are like that because they are not yet staggering around top-heavy with burdensome beliefs. If you take a child into a foreign country, the child will learn the language quickly, but not because they've got some kind of language program they have bought. It's because they are interacting— taking that small embarrassing step, over and over, getting it wrong and experiencing the new language with other children who speak it.

Most adults don't *ever* do that.

Adults like to retreat into an informational cocoon where they read books about the language and watch videos and listen to audios about the language. But notice how the going is painfully slow. It's not easy for them! This dense morass of information called a language!

When I was in the army, I went to the Defense Language Institute in Monterey, California, and for a year I studied Russian. It was very challenging. It was different than studying a language in college or high school because the army only wanted transformation. They wanted us to be able to *use* this language really well! (They told us our national security was at stake.)

They had us *interact* all day, only speaking Russian with our classmates and the teachers. We were always on the spot, challenged to the point of constant failure. Never a word of English! We had six different teachers each day and only six students per class. There was nowhere to hide. There was no comfort zone anywhere. Rumors were that they would take the lowest 20% of the class and flush them out of the school and send them into the fighting in Vietnam.

Learn or die?

Best motivation I ever had to convert information into transformation.

I once saw an ad on TV about some program where you could learn a foreign language "effortlessly." There was a really excited spokesperson doing the infomercial and he actually said, "All you have to do is *listen* and you learn the language."

Just put on these audio programs. Sit back and let the strange words filter and drift into your mind. Like fogging a bedroom full of wasps. Let the foggy mist of information saturate your sleepy brain and in no time at all you'll be speaking like a native.

False advertising! Buy their program and all you'll get is a headache.

The problem? There's no interaction. There's no testing. Only ongoing brain fog. There's no experimentation and there's no failure.

And failure is a must.

Failure is the way.

Being able to change into someone who can do something *surprisingly well* requires failure. You have to make a mistake to get to it. In learning a language you have to say the word the wrong way to really get the right way. You have to say something embarrassing to someone in Russian to laugh and correct yourself and get it right and really get it in your soul.

The same is true with anything I want to change for the better.

This is why people are addicted to information for so long. Because there's no possibility of failure in information-gathering. We can't really fail at that. We can do that forever. Most of the books in a library are books about other books. Useless information breeds and spreads itself all over the place.

I'm sitting down, overeating information, reading one more blog post. One more non-fatal overdose. But I myself won't change until I act. Until I get up and ask someone to dance.

10

You don't have to motivate yourself

People say to me, "How do I motivate myself to get better at this?"

Well, it isn't a matter of motivating yourself. It's a matter of doing small things. You can do them without motivation. Neither do you need inspiration or passion. We're just talking about a minute of your time. Or ten minutes or fifteen.

A simple choice. As easy as going into an ice cream store. Would you like chocolate ice cream or vanilla? It's just a choice. It's not as if I have to develop some kind of decision-making power before I choose chocolate or vanilla. I don't have to pump decision-making iron. It's just a choice.

This choosing thing seems almost too simple. Why make a big deal out of something that now looks really obvious to everyone? And the answer is: it is *not* obvious to everyone. It's so UNKNOWN that it's shocking.

I considered myself fairly enlightened and somewhat intelligent for years and years and I didn't even begin to see it. I did not see the choice I could make for transformation over information.

I kept adding more and more information and wondering why things didn't work out and then demonizing myself like,

"Well, you're not very persistent. You don't have the right kind of willpower, you don't have the courage, you don't have the stamina, you don't have the sense of purpose that other people do!"

And then I'd make up all these stories about myself that would put me in a bad light, that would make me feel even *less* like doing things. I never realized that I was the one telling the (entirely optional, arbitrary) stories. These were my bedtime stories I told myself each night to help me not sleep.

Later in life I found out that I was not alone. Most people do what I was doing. (Hence my choice of profession: I'll see if I can help other people see this!) People think learning to play the piano requires something amazing. They think becoming prosperous requires something extraordinary. And then they go running after the information they think they need for it!

And all this time, all it is, is a small choice. So I told myself: One minute. One freaking minute for God's sake.

FOURTEENTH CHOICE

Love vs. Fear

And I'll bury my soul in a scrapbook,
with the photographs there, and the moss.
And I'll yield to the flood of your beauty,
my cheap violin, and my cross.

~ **Leonard Cohen**
Take This Waltz

1

What do I fear might happen?

I can start my day with this question: "What would I love to do?" And then make my list of things.

Or I can start my day (as I did for years . . . no, decades) with, "What do I fear might happen today? What should I try to avoid?"

All these choices are versions of love versus fear. For example, when I choose transformation over information I am choosing a love of adventure and growth—versus fear of not knowing enough.

When I choose to live as a verb instead of a noun I am choosing an innate love of movement. A love of dancing with the universe. A joy I can take in motion and self-expression, versus the fear that pushes me into the corner where I learn to be a wallflower. I can bury my personality in a scrapbook and yield to the flood of life's beauty.

My friend, the author Lori Richards, likes to ask the question, "What would love do?" whenever she is unsure of her next action or communication. It's such a useful question! When choosing how to respond to that nasty email, or how to communicate with *anyone*, it's the perfect question. It leads me away from merely reacting. It leads me into the wonderful world of creating.

What would love do?

2

His journey was from fear to love

Brian Johnson is a friend, a teacher, and a force in the world. A force of nature! He has incomprehensible energy! Which he teaches all of us to have! He is the human embodiment of crazy good.

He is a young philosopher who teaches with compelling videos that I now urge you to find and watch. Find Brian Johnson. He has moved my life and the lives of so many of my friends and family members.

His own life has been a hero's journey, traveling from fear to love. He's journeyed from suicidal depression to inspiration and, finally, to a life in which he is prospering from doing what he loves the most. A life of love and intellectual adventure.

You can watch a compelling account of Brian's journey from fear to love when you watch the movie *Finding Joe*. It's a film about the legendary Joseph Campbell, and Brian is unforgettable in it.

Brian shook my world a while back when he sent me this quotation from Friedrich Nietzsche:

This is the manner of noble souls: they do not want to have anything for nothing; least of all, life. Whoever is of the mob wants to live for nothing; we others, however, to whom life gave itself, we always think about what we might best give in return . . . One should not wish to enjoy where one does not give joy.

Brian gives joy. To all those who watch his teaching, to the readers of his enlightening book *Philosopher's Notes*, and to me.

Like when he sent me that white lab coat and goggles one day.

He wanted to emphasize the value of experimentation. People can talk to me about the value of a life of experimentation, but only Brian would send me goggles and a lab coat to wear.

I'm wearing them now. As I write this sentence.

Because Brian's the first person I think of when I'm thinking crazy good.

The quote he sent me by Nietzsche left me all shook up. In a good way. It was a wakeup call. Especially where Nietzsche says we should not wish to enjoy and not *give joy back*.

A life well-lived gives us joy. Why would we not give joy in return?

Since reading the quote and since meeting Brian I have been completely high-stepping, even moonwalking on the road from fear to love. The crazy-good road. That road less traveled. It is *joy-giving*, plain and simple. That's all there is. Success follows, but that's not the primary reason to do it. The primary reason is in the doing itself, and how it moves the soul along.

Brian Johnson says his success in the world, which is extraordinary, is based on his "being willing to put on the lab coat and the goggles and go get to work."

Every day Brian draws a little lightning bolt in his journal. That represents astonishment and the concept of crazy good.

(Creating something *way* better than it has to be. Creating something that is going to surprise people. Something that's not merely good.)

After he draws his lightning bolt he asks himself how he can serve profoundly today, this day, and create extraordinary value. He says, "I so enjoy coming back to that ruthless focus . . . well, how do I make today a masterpiece? Like, truly, what would a masterpiece day look like? And then I want to celebrate each incremental step in the direction of creating a masterpiece throughout the day. This has been a really, really fun practice."

3

Learning to love what is

For years I've heard people recommend that I learn to *love what is*. I even recorded an audio program myself called "Welcoming Every Circumstance." I've read with pleasure as gurus have written that I should see the opportunity inside each problem.

But I've never heard of anyone applying that philosophy as obsessively (and effectively) as Jonathan Keyser.

Keyser is chairman and CEO of the most visionary, progressive commercial real estate company in the land. He is a passionate advocate for basing a business on profound, relentless, disruptive (to the industry sclerosis) service.

A few months ago he issued a thirty-day challenge to his company and all its fans and followers. This is what it was: For thirty days each one of us will *see the gift in everything*. If anything looks like "bad news" and not a gift, we are to stop and list three reasons why it is actually a gift.

His people had a blast. But there was struggle and challenge, too, throughout the thirty days. Because not everything *looks like* a gift. At first. We've been heavily conditioned to make most unexpected circumstances look threatening to us. We save our best radar for the bad news. So the challenge was liberating. Especially because it was taken and applied in the real world—the exciting and complex lurid carnival of business and street smarts.

Most people do this kind of visualization on a yoga mat or at a mountain retreat, where the challenges can all be hypothetical. Mind stuff. Pure imagination.

In contrast to that, Jonathan continuously implements a living, practical, wildly-successful vision. It is occurring in real time in the real world, with real people feeling real joy because they are joy-giving.

4

The not so serious life

Fear is what leads to a life of expectations, the need for life and other people to be (and *behave*) a certain way. For me to be happy.

Love, on the other hand, is behind the creation of an agreement. An agreement is like a co-written song.

Love can build a bridge between your heart and mine.

My friend, the songwriter-musician Peter Sykes, offered to write a theme song (as a pure musical gift) for an internet video show I've been doing with Jason Goldberg called *The Not So Serious Life*. Because I so *loved* doing this show (about how to not take things so seriously), I immediately wrote these suggested first lyrics for Peter's song:

> Are you tired of . . . pain and strife?
> Your angry husband
> Or furious wife?
> Then come with us to a show you'll like:
> *The Not So Serious Life.*

This whole life of mine is now one big show. The greatest show on earth.

5

The shorter story: no love, no glory

I saw a photo of a subway underpass tunnel with bold graffiti on the wall that said, "FEAR IS A LIAR."

It was spray-painted for all who passed through to see. (Paul Simon predicted this. He said the words of the prophets would be written on the subway walls.)

I had to think awhile about that FEAR IS A LIAR graffiti before the truth of it really hit me. I saw it was true. Fear lies to me all day. It tells me it's always safer to try to be safe. It tells me that creative self-expression is risky. Fear tells me I always need other people's approval. It tells me I need to win friends and influence as many people as I can. Fear tells me to make sure my shaky reputation holds together. That's what fear does.

Love, on the other hand, is not a liar.

It is a glorious truth-teller. Where there is love, there is glory. Love spirals up into creativity, like a flower flourishing upward. Emmet Fox famously wrote, "If you could only love enough, you'd be the most powerful person in the world."

I see that. I'm always more powerful when fear is replaced by love.

For example, I used to fear a life without drugs and alcohol. I used to fear any form of socializing or "being me" out in the world without a lot of alcohol in my system.

Even during my first weeks and months in recovery, going to meetings, I was still living in fear. One of my fellow alcoholics in one of those early first meetings expressed this situation of first being sober (or "dry," maybe I should say) by saying, "The monkey's off my back, but the circus is still in town." Yes! I felt that!

But little by little my fear was being replaced by love. I began to love the meetings. And then I began to love the people in the meetings. I began to love being clear and sober. I loved the return of my brain to me. I could read things and remember them. I could breathe again, I could breathe in life. I was filled with love and it was real. Fear had been a liar.

It told me I couldn't live without it.

FIFTEENTH CHOICE

Living vs. Dying

Loving's really living.
Without it, you're not living, boy,
you're just getting up each day
and walking around.

~ Ian Tyson
The Loving Sound

1

A podcast host was interviewing me

A podcast host was interviewing me about some book I had written.

He wanted to know how I wanted to be remembered.

I asked him, "Why would I want to be remembered?"

Is there no end to our desire to impress other people? Does it get so obsessive that I even want to keep doing it after death?

He said, "What legacy do you want to leave?"

I said, "Open minds. Clear minds. No trace of me."

2

I saw the news today, oh boy

In the house across the street, someone is helping her friend recover from alcoholism. That will not make the news today.

They are sitting on a couch and talking gently about the steps of recovery and what it means to live one day at a time. The wild, affirming rain hits their window.

A life is being changed for the better. Gentle hope is replacing depression.

Now I turn my head a little, away from the picture window, and I stare at the TV screen next to the window and someone is beheading someone who doesn't agree with their religion. I am stunned. What am I to learn? What are the depths of human cowardice? Oh well. News, sports and weather are just trying to make a buck. It's been proven, it's been measured: ratings go up whenever the viewers feel threatened. Demetri Martin says all TV news shows should be called *What's Wrong.* Good evening! And welcome to the six o'clock edition of *What's Wrong!*

But if I shift my eyes back away from the screen a bit I can see the house across the street again. I enjoy realizing that something very beautiful is happening in that house and no one knows it because it is not on television. Across the street I see the choice that has to come before all the other choices. The choice for living.

It's later that night. Now the sun has gone down. And I hear the sirens as I lie in bed. The sounds of the city. Before crazy good, the sirens bothered me. I would always think they meant trouble. Someone is hurt. Some crash has happened. Someone is being rushed to the hospital. The sirens were sad to hear.

But now the sirens are comforting . . . relaxing. They reassure me. They are the sound of someone helping someone else.

Everything's a Godsend.

What else could it be?

Acknowledgments

To the inspiration for this book, John Vehr.

To creative consultant Fred Knipe.

To the ultimate coach, Steve Hardison.

To Kathy, for bringing me the sun . . . and making me smile.

To the ACS, you know who you are.

To our publisher, Maurice Bassett.

To Brian Johnson for the wisdom, the goggles and the lab coat.

To Jason Goldberg for the not so serious life.

To Byron Katie for the questions.

To Roxann Burroughs for the openings in my mind.

To Dicken Bettinger for explaining the principles.

To Terry Hill for Santa Anita.

To Nick Garboushian for Pablo Neruda and Tai Chi.

To Carrie Brito for the wonderful artwork.

To Bobby Baffert for the experience of Dortmund.

About the author

Steve Chandler has written dozens of books on subjects that swing dizzyingly from Jane Austen to baseball to business coaching to travel to obituaries to Moby Dick. He is the author of the bestsellers *Crazy Good* and *Time Warrior*.

Steve is the creator of the world-acclaimed Coaching Prosperity School and its Advanced Client Systems programs, now available as an online masterclass; find more information at www.stevechandler.com.

He lives in Birmingham, Michigan, with his wife and editor, Kathy, and two hell hounds.

Books by Steve Chandler

CREATOR
RIGHT NOW
Death Wish
Crazy Good
37 Ways to BOOST Your Coaching Practice
Wealth Warrior
Time Warrior
The Life Coaching Connection
Fearless
The Woman Who Attracted Money
Shift Your Mind Shift the World (revised edition)
17 Lies That Are Holding You Back
10 Commitments to Your Success
Reinventing Yourself
The Story of You
100 Ways to Motivate Yourself
How to Get Clients (revised edition)
50 Ways to Create Great Relationships
The Joy of Selling
Powerful Graceful Success
RelationShift (with Michael Bassoff)
The Small Business Millionaire (with Sam Beckford)
100 Ways to Create Wealth (with Sam Beckford)
9 Lies That Are Holding Your Business Back
(with Sam Beckford)
Business Coaching (with Sam Beckford)
100 Ways to Motivate Others (with Scott Richardson)
The Hands Off Manager (with Duane Black)
Two Guys On the Road (with Terrence Hill)

Two Guys Read the Box Scores (with Terrence Hill)
Two Guys Read Jane Austen (with Terrence Hill)
Two Guys Read Moby Dick (with Terrence Hill)
Two Guys Read the Obituaries (with Terrence Hill)
The Prosperous Coach (with Rich Litvin)

Audio by Steve Chandler

9 Lies That Are Holding Your Business Back
10 Habits of Successful Salespeople
17 Sales Lies
37 Ways to BOOST Your Coaching Practice (audiobook)
Are You A Doer Or A Feeler?
Challenges
Choosing
Crazy Good (audiobook)
CREATOR (audiobook)
Creating Clients
Creative Relationships
Death Wish (audiobook)
Expectation vs. Agreement
Fearless (audiobook)
Financially Fearless
How To Double Your Income As A Coach
How to Get Clients (revised edition) (audiobook)
How To Help A Pessimist
How To Solve Problems
Information vs. Transformation
Is It A Dream Or A Project?
Making A Difference
MindShift: The Steve Chandler Success Course
Ownership And Leadership
People People
Personality Reinvented
Purpose vs. Personality
Reflections on RelationShift: Major-Gift Fundraising
RIGHT NOW (audiobook)

Serving vs. Pleasing People
Shift Your Mind Shift the World (revised edition) (audiobook)
Testing vs. Trusting
The Creating Wealth audio series
The Fearless Mindset
The Focused Leader
The Function Of Optimism
The Joy Of Succeeding
The Most Powerful Client Attractor
The Owner / Victim Choice
The Prosperous Coach (audiobook)
The Ultimate Time Management System
Time Warrior (audiobook)
Wealth Warrior (audiobook)
Welcoming Every Circumstance
Who You Know vs. What You Do
Why Should I Reinvent Myself?
You'll Get What You Want By Asking For It

Steve Chandler Coaching Prosperity School

Steve's world-acclaimed ACS (Advanced Client Systems) is now available as an online masterclass at a tenth of the cost of the original program.

Check out all the features and content of the *Steve Chandler Coaching Prosperity School* on Steve's website, www.stevechandler.com

- Learn to convert your coaching skills into prosperity.
- Hear our powerful guest teachers share their insights and secrets to getting clients and creating a financially thriving practice.
- You'll learn from Steve Chandler and great coaches like Rich Litvin, Carolyn Freyer-Jones, Michael Neill, Karen Davis, Ron Wilder and many more . . . all graduates of the Coaching Prosperity School.
- Over 30 full video lessons and more than 50 short video tips, plus bonus audio programs to build your coaching practice.

"This man has changed—and continues to change—my life! One of the reasons that I am the coach I am today is because of his wisdom and leadership.

"Seeing him model masterful coaching and transformational living and practice building through the Coaching Prosperity School program was one of the most insightful and empowering experiences of my life.

"If you are a coach who is committed to greatness in building your practice without internet marketing tactics or having to have a huge mailing list or Twitter followers, AND get the results from yourself that are required to truly be prosperous, being a part of Steve Chandler's new program may be the greatest investment you ever make in yourself."

~ **Jason Goldberg,** master coach and author of *Prison Break*

GO HERE to learn more:

www.stevechandler.com

Publisher's Catalogue

The Prosperous Series

#1 The Prosperous Coach: Increase Income and Impact for You and Your Clients (Steve Chandler and Rich Litvin)

#2 The Prosperous Hip Hop Producer: My Beat-Making Journey from My Grandma's Patio to a Six-Figure Business (Curtiss King)

#3 The Prosperous Hotelier (David Lund)

* * *

Devon Bandison

Fatherhood Is Leadership: Your Playbook for Success, Self-Leadership, and a Richer Life

Roy G. Biv

Dancing on Rainbows: A Celebration of Numismatic Art

Sir Fairfax L. Cartwright

The Mystic Rose from the Garden of the King

Steve Chandler

37 Ways to BOOST Your Coaching Practice: PLUS: the 17 Lies That Hold Coaches Back and the Truth That Sets Them Free

50 Ways to Create Great Relationships

Business Coaching (Steve Chandler and Sam Beckford)

Crazy Good: A Book of CHOICES

CREATOR

Death Wish: The Path through Addiction to a Glorious Life

Fearless: Creating the Courage to Change the Things You Can

How to Get Clients (Revised Edition)

The Prosperous Coach: Increase Income and Impact for You and Your Clients (The Prosperous Series #1) (Steve Chandler and Rich Litvin)

RIGHT NOW: Mastering the Beauty of the Present Moment

Shift Your Mind Shift The World (Revised Edition)

Time Warrior: How to defeat procrastination, people-pleasing, self-doubt, over-commitment, broken promises and chaos

Wealth Warrior: The Personal Prosperity Revolution

Kazimierz Dąbrowski

Positive Disintegration

Charles Dickens

A Christmas Carol: A Special Full-Color, Fully-Illustrated Edition

Melissa Ford

Living Service: The Journey of a Prosperous Coach

James F. Gesualdi

Excellence Beyond Compliance: Enhancing Animal Welfare Through the Constructive Use of the Animal Welfare Act

Janice Goldman

Let's Talk About Money: The Girlfriends' Guide to Protecting Her ASSets

Sylvia Hall

This Is Real Life: Love Notes to Wake You Up

Christy Harden

Guided by Your Own Stars: Connect with the Inner Voice and Discover Your Dreams

I ♥ Raw: A How-To Guide for Reconnecting to Yourself and the Earth through Plant-Based Living

Curtiss King

The Prosperous Hip Hop Producer: My Beat-Making Journey from My Grandma's Patio to a Six-Figure Business (The Prosperous Series #2)

David Lindsay

A Blade for Sale: The Adventures of Monsieur de Mailly

David Lund

The Prosperous Hotelier (The Prosperous Series #3)

Abraham H. Maslow

The Aims of Education (audio)

The B-language Workshop (audio)

Being Abraham Maslow (DVD)

The Eupsychian Ethic (audio)

The Farther Reaches of Human Nature (audio)

Maslow and Self-Actualization (DVD)

Maslow on Management (audiobook)

Personality and Growth: A Humanistic Psychologist in the Classroom

Psychology and Religious Awareness (audio)

The Psychology of Science: A Reconnaissance

Self-Actualization (audio)

Weekend with Maslow (audio)

Harold E. Robles

Albert Schweitzer: An Adventurer for Humanity

Albert Schweitzer

Reverence for Life: The Words of Albert Schweitzer

William Tillier

Personality Development through Positive Disintegration: The Work of Kazimierz Dąbrowski

Margery Williams

The Velveteen Rabbit: or How Toys Become Real

Join our Mailing List:
www.MauriceBassett.com

MAURICE BASSETT
books for athletes of the mind